PREACHERS WITH POWER

PREACHERS WITH POWER

Four Stalwarts of The South

Douglas F. Kelly

THE BANNER OF TRUTH TRUST

THE BANNER OF TRUTH TRUST
3 Murrayfield Road, Edinburgh EH12 6EL
PO Box 621, Carlisle, Pennsylvania 17013, USA

*

First published 1992
ISBN 0 85151 628 9

*

Typeset in 11/12 pt. Baskerville
at The Spartan Press Limited, Lymington, Hants
and printed in Great Britain by
St Edmundsbury Press Ltd,
Bury St Edmunds, Suffolk

To
my mother,
Lucy Martha Pate Kelly,

whose great-grandfather, Willis Pate, served in the 23rd South Carolina Volunteers along with John L. Girardeau during the War Between the States;

and to the memory of my father,
Floyd Ferguson Kelly,

both of whose parents were brought up under the preaching of their mutual cousin, the Rev. Martin McQueen, in Moore County, North Carolina. 'Father McQueen', as he was popularly known, had studied under B. M. Palmer at Columbia Seminary and had sat under the frequent preaching of J. H. Thornwell in the First Presbyterian Church of Columbia in the mid-1850s. His ministry was deeply marked by theirs, and he in turn influenced for decades my father's parents and grandparents on both maternal and paternal sides.

'*Know therefore that the Lord thy God, he is God, the faithful God, which keepeth covenant and mercy with them that love him and keep his commandments to a thousand generations*' Deuteronomy 7:9.

CONTENTS

PREFACE

The substance of the chapters of this small volume on Thornwell, Palmer and Girardeau was originally delivered as speeches at the opening Pastoral Conference of Greenville Theological Seminary in Greenville, South Carolina, in May 1987. I am grateful to Duncan Rankin, my friend and former student assistant, for having originally suggested these topics (and for having collected some appropriate pictures in Charleston, South Carolina, for the subsequent book). I also appreciate the kindness which Professor Morton H. Smith and Elder and Mrs J. Ligon Duncan II of Greenville showed to me during that pleasant time. Later, the Rev. Iain H. Murray suggested that I add a chapter on Daniel Baker, which I did during my sabbatical leave in Edinburgh in 1988. The staff of the Presbyterian Historical Foundation in Montreat, North Carolina, helpfully sent me needed material on Baker.

Many other people have significantly helped me in editing and otherwise preparing this book. Several of my students at the Reformed Theological Seminary in Jackson, Mississippi, should be mentioned: John Koelling and Mike Forester, who served as my student assistants before their graduation in May 1990, ably transposed this material from the typewriter to the computer, and helped in other ways; another student friend, Jon Balserak, helped with some of the computer work; John Morrow, my former student assistant, has made many trips for me and helped in various ways, as has another student friend, Larry Rountree. More recently, Russ Ragon, my present student assistant, has been in charge of incorporating the final necessary changes before going to press.

In the early stages of this work, I had some fruitful discussions with Dr John Reed Miller, long-time pastor of First Presbyterian Church in Jackson before his retirement. I was privileged to be his summer assistant in 1966, and since that time I have never ceased to learn from him. In particular, I owe the title of this book to him.

The Rev. Iain Murray has offered a number of suggestions, which have, I think, strengthened the text. Mr James ('Sonny') Peaster of Yazoo City, Mississippi, has also assisted in this project by carefully working through the whole manuscript and making helpful suggestions. My colleague, Dr Albert H. Freundt, Professor of Church History at the Reformed Theological Seminary of Jackson, graciously gave me some valuable bibliographical assistance, especially dealing with events in Savannah and New Orleans. Dr Luder Whitlock, President of the Reformed Theological Seminary, has also been of encouragement and assistance in this project in many ways.

Finally, my son, Angus Robertson Kelly III, let me do much of the original typing in his room (for a small fee!), when my study was being used as a guest room. My best friend and assistant in this writing project – as in all others – has been my wife, Caroline. She has done a great deal of final editing of the entire material.

I offer sincerest thanks to all of these kind friends.

DOUGLAS KELLY

Jackson, Mississippi, 1991

THE OLD SOUTH: AN INTRODUCTION

This volume offers a consideration of the lives, and particularly the preaching, of four servants of God, who lived between the years 1791 and 1902 in the Southeastern Atlantic states of America, more popularly known as 'the Old South'. Although our focus is primarily on spiritual and eternal issues rather than historical and cultural questions, it nevertheless seems appropriate to take a brief look at the significance of the Southern culture as a whole. After all, that is the context in which Baker, Thornwell, Palmer and Girardeau served 'their generation by the will of God'. It is also evident that the Old South will be far removed in time, space and ethos from many who may read these pages in other lands and continents.

'The South' is both a place and a state of mind. Geographically speaking, the Southern States of America begin with Virginia in the North. They run South through the two Carolinas, down the Atlantic coast to Georgia, Alabama and Florida, then turn West through Mississippi and Louisiana to Texas. Tennessee, directly West of North Carolina, and once a part of it, is also a part of the South, as is Arkansas, which joins it. These were the major *Confederate* states during the War of Secession in the early 1860s. Border states, such as Maryland and Kentucky, have historically had some Southern affinities but were not really a part of the Old South.

This area was the first part of the American continent to be colonized by Britain. In 1585, Sir Walter Raleigh made an unsuccessful attempt to establish a settlement on what is now

Roanoke Island in North Carolina. Then, in 1612, some twenty-seven years later and some hundred miles to the North, settlers founded Jamestown, Virginia. They named the young colony after Queen Elizabeth, the Virgin Queen, and Jamestown for England's reigning monarch, King James I. Over the next century, Virginia greatly prospered as a trading, cultural and religious outpost of England. Other colonists came to Carolina, which was granted a royal charter in 1663. Charleston (then known as Charlestown, for King Charles II) was founded in 1670 as part of the new colony of South Carolina.

By the early and mid-eighteenth century, the growing population of these three states pushed South and Westward as the Indians were moved back and new lands opened up for settlement. As a result, most landholding families in Mississippi and Alabama today are descendants of Virginia and Carolina people. Often it was the younger children in a family who traveled west because they did not inherit the parental land. By this time, also, the French had an important settlement in Louisiana, which was the only significant non-Anglo-Saxon portion of the Old South.

We have spoken of the South not only as a geographical location but also as a state of mind. The origin of that mentality lies in the type of people who filled the coastal plains, foothills and mountains of the region. The vast majority were people of British origin who began settling these Southern colonies nearly one hundred years after the great Protestant Reformation. With them came the effects of the Reformation that had re-established two important tenets of the faith: the Bible as the final authority of faith and practice, and justification by faith in Christ's finished work as the only way of salvation. Indeed, the Carolinas and Virginia were being settled during the English Puritan movement that brought the biblical doctrines of grace to the fore. Several directors of the Virginia Company (Sir Edwin Sandys, for instance) were of Puritan sympathies, although they, unlike other Puritans known as Brownists, did not think it necessary to separate from the official Church of England.

While most of the earlier Southern colonists left Europe more for economic reasons than did the Pilgrims and Puritans of New England (who came more specifically to set up 'a church in the wilderness' according to the pattern shown them 'in the mount'), nonethelcss they all came out of the Reformation and Puritan context. The Virginia Charter specifically stated that while the colony was intended to make an economic profit and to extend the authority of the King of England, it was also to spread the blessings of the gospel of Christ to the natives in accordance with the Great Commission of Matthew, chapter 28. Thus, although the economic and political motives were significant, there is no reason to doubt that most officials and settlers of the Old South saw themselves as Protestant Christians, who, in developing the new territories, would also glorify God by establishing churches and spreading the Reformed faith.

At the risk of serious over-simplification, we might say that, while many English settlers secured the finest plantation land in the coastal plains of the upper and mid-Southern states, Scotch-Irish and large groups of Highland Scots settled the 'upcountry' areas that had generally less rich soil. These areas included the Piedmont and mountainous regions, and particularly the Cape Fear Valley of North Carolina. As a result, the classicil plantation culture of the South tended to be in these wealthy coastal areas settled by well-to-do gentry, especially in the 'Tidewater' of Virginia, 'Low Country' South Carolina and parts of Maryland. It is here that a genteel social life flourished in elegant Georgian houses such as Drayton Hall near Charleston, or Greek-Revival mansions like Orton Plantation near Wilmington, North Carolina, surrounded by huge, broad fields, worked by hundreds of slaves. These Low Country people were generally Anglican, and in the earlier years commonly sent their sons to be educated in either Old or New England. Only after the 1820s did they begin to patronize their own Southern state universities and religious colleges.

In comparison the plainer, more middle-class Scottish and Northern-Irish population typically lived on smaller plots of land, such as the hundred-acre farms in Moore County, North Carolina, or Danville, Virginia, and had fewer (or no) slaves. None the less, because of their Presbyterian Reformation background, the upcountry population tended to be very educationally minded and biblically very literate. These solid farm people established record numbers of schools, academies and colleges. Most of these had some kind of connection with various Presbyterian judicatories, though they were nearly always open to, and patronized by, every denomination in the community.

The famous (or perhaps notorious) rabidly Southern novelist, Thomas Dixon (author of such stories as *The Clansman*, from which was taken the influential film of the 1920s, 'The Birth of a Nation') often refers in his novels to this cultural difference between low-country English aristocracy and up-country Celtic middle class. It is his opinion that the 'true blue Southerners' are the Celts! Recent historical studies have also argued that much of the character of the Old South is to be explained by its Celtic origins. They cite as examples the wild military charges under General 'Stonewall' Jackson during the War Between the States, or the common preference for leisure, good food and drink as opposed to the stiff efforts required to make economic progress. However, it must be said that while such ideas are interesting, they concern matters that are difficult to quantify and impossible to prove.

It is clear that various types of the plantation system all formed the economic and cultural base in which the mind of the Old South was developed. As a result, from the late seventeenth century until the 1950s or even 1960s, the South remained an agrarian economy with largely rural values and folkways, shaped by strong elements of evangelical Christianity especially since the First Great Awakening of the 1730s and 1740s. At the same time, 'worldly' practices, such as cock-fighting, gambling, heavy drinking and duelling were not unknown among many of the planters and others.

This plantation or farm basis of the Southern culture and mind has had several important consequences. First, many hands were needed to clear the forests and then to work the fields, which meant that large numbers of children were desirable. Large families were thus the norm in the South with the result that the entire culture has tended to be pervaded by a sense of kinship, family history and family-centered thinking and activity. While, of course, large numbers of children were common across the world in the eighteenth and nineteenth centuries, the South had its own unique form of 'extended family', with several sons or nephews living in different houses on the same plantation, or at least in the same area.

These family interconnections among the different plantations (including not infrequent intermarriages between distant cousins) played a major social, political and religious role in the culture. For example, in the Old South, it was often of more consequence to be kin to certain people than to be wealthy. The effect of these large extended families could be seen in church life also. Numbers of rural churches with congregations of perhaps three or four hundred members might have only six or seven different surnames. Family members, for six or seven straight generations, would be buried either in family graveyards on the plantations or more often in family plots in the long rows of tombs surrounding the rural, white wooden church.

All these factors were part of a patriarchal vision of society and gave rise to generations of people with a deep sense of family roots, shared heritage, and belonging to one another and to the land. This patriarchal mentality of the South coexisted with an almost mystical sense of the value of family land and the preciousness of continuing to live in the same place generation after generation.

Even with the large families there was still a great need for farm labor, which meant that there was a ready market for the black slaves. Slave-traders from England and New England brought these West Africans by way of the West Indies. In the early years of the Old South, slavery was generally considered acceptable throughout both the British Empire and most of the world. By the nineteenth century, a more biblically compassionate and sensitive consciousness existed in much of the Western world, so that slave-trading and slavery came to be abolished except in the Southern United States. It was on the issue of slavery that the Southern mind tended to deviate and to stand at a distance from the norm of ethical values later to be found in other Christian lands.

Competent studies (such as *Slavery and Sectionalism* by John Akers) have demonstrated that until the early 1820s there was considerable openness in the Old South toward realizing the evil of slavery and a strong interest in eventually ending it. While we cannot enter into a study of slavery here, we should point out that most Southerners held to a view of domestic servitude in which they felt that the slave was in some sense a member of the larger family circle, with commensurate duties and privileges. For example, the correspondence of the distinguished Southern Presbyterian minister Charles C. Jones with his son is permeated with a sense of family attachment and affection for his bondmen. (These letters are gathered under the title: *A Georgian at Princeton*[1]). This family atmosphere is further illustrated in an incidental reference by James W. Alexander, son of Professor Archibald Alexander of Princeton (1772–1851), in *Thoughts on Family Worship*. He describes how the drawing rooms and passages of a Virginia plantation house belonging to his cousins were filled with both family members and black slaves at morning worship. Side by side, they sang the melodious praises of God, and then knelt together in prayer before they faced the tasks of the day.

The carefully researched historical work of Dr Robert L. Dabney in *A Defense of Virginia, and through her of the South*,[2] is instructive in demonstrating the difference in attitude of the evangelical Southerner toward domestic servitude and the kind of slavery practiced, let us say, in the Arab world. Rightly or wrongly, the Christians of the South believed that their form was related to the domestic bondage of the Old Testament. And the Southern viewpoint on the family nature of their 'peculiar institution' is also brought out clearly in a letter of December 10, 1856, from James H. Thornwell to John B. Adger. In this letter, Thornwell states why he is strongly opposed to the re-opening of the slave-trade in the United States (which some Southern politicians were discussing at the time):

> My judgment and my feelings are decidedly opposed to the slave trade, in every respect in which the subject can be viewed, and I am sorry that it has been agitated at all. In the first place, it would change the whole character of the institution, as it exists amongst us. It is now domestic and patriarchal; the slave has all the family associations, and family pride, and sympathies of the master. He is born in the house, and bred with the children. The sentiments which spring from this circumstance, in the master and the slave, soften all the asperities of the relation, and secure obedience as a sort of filial respect. This humanizing element would be lost, the moment we cease to rear our slaves, and rely upon a foreign market . . .[3]

Even with the most optimistic assessment of this institution (which was, of course, from the viewpoint of the owner, not of the slave), many Southern Christians – perhaps even a majority – wished to end slave-trading immediately, and slavery eventually. However, because of the rise of abolitionism, the debates surrounding the Missouri Compromise of 1819–20 and two slave rebellions, the Southern mind became extremely defensive over this issue and closed itself off from the criticism and advice of its naturally closest and truest friends in other countries. For example, in the 1840s, the Old School Presbyterian Church stoutly closed its ears to pleas asking it to reconsider its position on human bondage from its very close physical and theological cousin, the Free Church of Scotland, a previously honored and trusted sister church.

Before we look at the tragic outcome of the South's intransigence on slavery and related issues, we must consider a second feature of the plantation/agrarian-based society. To this day, the Southern states are culturally and religiously different from the Northern and Western parts of the United States because they were not significantly influenced by the massive immigration movements of the late nineteenth and early twentieth centuries. At that time, literally millions of people from Southern and Eastern Europe with Roman Catholic and Jewish heritage poured into the North. Prior to the 1850s, most of the young American Republic had a Protestant and biblical base of thought and culture. We do not mean that most people were personally regenerate, or even church members, but their modes of thought and their basic institutions rested on Christian foundations. The massive immigrations from more Catholic and secularist areas of Europe severely eroded the biblical and reformational base of much of the North, Northeast and Western areas of the country. For example, Congregational Massachusetts became largely Irish Catholic, and formerly Dutch Reformed, Anglican and Presbyterian New York became an amalgam of Italian Catholic, Polish, Russian and German Jewish and various other groups. Not a few of these later immigrants had also been touched by secularist strands of thought which came from the French Enlightenment.

Such changes did not occur in the unindustrialized South, because the new immigrants went to areas where there was work in mills and plants, and the South had no place for them.

Its land had already been parceled out for generations, and its farm labor was carried out by both white and black tenants and sharecroppers. The net result was that the South was more able to retain its biblical-traditional basis of thought and its British and African racial and cultural predominance. There was far less of a cultural and historical divide between a typical Southern family in 1830 and 1930 than there was between a typical New Jersey, Connecticut or Michigan family during the same period. That may explain, in part, the Northern sense of surprise at how the typical Southerner (to their way of thought) 'lives in the past'. To the Southern mind, the Mississippi novelist, William Faulkner, was speaking with an element of truth, when he said: 'the past is not past; it is present.'

As far as this volume of studies is concerned, the most valuable heritage that was passed down from the early South to the present was Bible-based, evangelical Christianity, little touched by non-reformational and secularist streams of thought which accompanied the later immigrants. But merely to pass down the formularies and symbols of a traditional faith can bring ossification and skeptical reaction, as seems to have happened in the late seventeenth- and early eighteenth-century German Lutheran 'orthodoxy'. The form of sound words has ever to be accompanied by a vital stream of life and love, and that stream of living waters with life and love from a higher world did periodically overflow in the traditional orthodox churches of the South in times of large-scale revival.

Later in this volume (especially in the chapters on John L. Girardeau and Daniel Baker) we shall discuss in some detail the times and characteristics of these revivals. The record shows that the religion of the preponderant majority, including both the leadership and the 'working' classes was renewed, purified, invigorated and extended through three great periods of outpouring of the Holy Spirit: the First Great Awakening (during the 1740s), the Second Great Awakening (from the 1780s to the 1830s) and the 1858/59 Revival, which continued in the Confederate army from about 1861 to 1863. Hence, the evangelical Christianity of the South (whether Baptist, Presbyterian, Methodist and, to some degree, even Anglican) is revival Christianity.

Certain characteristics commonly found in all these denominations can be summarized as follows: a stress on personal dealings with a holy and gracious God; the seriousness of sin; the greatness of God's love in the gospel; the one way of salvation through a personal, believing appropriation of the atoning blood of Jesus Christ; the reality of heaven and hell; the brevity of life and the need to be ready for eternity; the necessity of bearing the fruit of the Spirit and of standing against sin (though this has tended to be defined more in individualist than in societal terms); the importance of the disciplines of personal piety; the full inspiration of Scripture and the need to maintain the fundamentals of the faith against all forms of soul-destroying secularism and modernism. Such have been the standards sought by the Southern churches, although it must be added that they have often failed to attain and exemplify them, especially during this present century, which has experienced as yet no major revival.

Distinguished scholars of Southern culture such as Dr Samuel S. Hill of the University of Florida, and Dr John S. Reed of the University of North Carolina) have pointed out that evangelical Christianity is the religion of most of the population of the South. This is in direct contrast with all the other regions of the nation, which are dominated either by liberal Protestantism, Roman Catholicism or some form of materialist secularism. Nor has there ever been a serious alternative form of religion to challenge the evangelical preponderance of the South, not even the skeptical Deism emanating from the European Enlightenment, which was largely swept away by the Second Great Awakening. How this matter stands at present is a question to which we must shortly return.

Undoubtedly, the ideal of revival Christianity which has been held up in the Southern churches has had much to do with the cultivation and continuation of traditional Southern virtues. The South is still known for hospitality, personal courtesy, generally quiet and calm manners in public, and the saying of 'Sir' and 'Ma'am' by children to adults. When this writer from the rural South first began traveling and living abroad as a student nearly twenty-five years ago, on meeting fellow citizens of the United States in European railway stations and public places, he could often immediately identify the Southerners as compared to the 'Yankees'. There tended to be a certain difference in bearing, in tone of voice and at times in general approach to the surroundings. But today there is probably less difference than there was a quarter of a century ago.

Evangelical orthodoxy and personal courtesy are the bright sides of the Southern mind at its very best. But it also has a darker side. Since it is considered a virtue to hold strong convictions, Southerners have perhaps been too ready to fight on occasions when negotiation would have been entirely possible. At times also, it has tended to engender a certain sense of feeling set apart, if not superior, which can all too easily degenerate into a kind of narrow provincialism, blind to its own faults. This has been most notably the case in the South's poor record in race relations and in its not infrequent inclination toward clannishness, snobbery, gossip and jealousy. Presumably, other regions are just as bad in some or all these sins, but given its evangelical privileges, people from outside have quite properly expected better from a region with such orthodox churches and large Sunday attendance.

The most positive construction that one could put upon these intermittent glaring inconsistencies would be to recognize the continuance of 'indwelling sin' (see Romans 7), and the imperfection of the believer's sanctification in this earthly life. We must not forget either that nominal Christianity, even in orthodox churches, is generally more common than true spirituality, but we will leave the final adjudication of these matters to the Last Day.

What we must consider here, although in brief compass, is that great historical divide in Southern history: the Civil War (historically referred to in the South as the War Between the States) and the complex of painful, moral and political controversies which led up to it. We will briefly summarize the constitutional and political issues resulting in the 1861 Secession of the South from the Union and the formation of the Confederate States of America.

In the first place, the Northern and Midwestern states had begun to outnumber the Southern states by the late 1820s and were not averse to using their greater voting power in Congress for their own economic interests.

The Northern states were rapidly becoming industrialized, and thus opposed international free trade for the Southern states in order to grant protection to their own industries, by using the South as a source of cheap raw materials and a plentiful market outlet. The agrarian economy of the rural South naturally preferred free trade rather than protected markets, for often their raw products (such as cotton and tobacco) brought more in England and France than in New York or Philadelphia, while British and French finished products might well be cheaper and more elegant than those of Massachusetts or New Jersey. Sheldon Vanauken has summarized clearly the conflicting interests of the mid-nineteenth century American Republic: 'the North was for empire; the South for independence', for 'an industrial democracy was opposing the interests of an agrarian aristocracy.'[4]

This economic conflict crystalized in the Tariff and Nullification Controversy, which nearly split the Union in the early 1830s. The Northern states (which by then could command a majority in Congress) imposed a tariff on foreign goods against the will of the South, effectively raising the prices of finished products for Southerners while at the same time prejudicing European markets against their lifeline: the raw products of cotton, rice and tobacco. South Carolina promptly nullified this tariff, and after threats of invasion of that state by President Andrew Jackson, a compromise was reached and the tariff was dropped. But hostile feelings and mutual suspicion remained.

Later in the decade, the rise of fervent abolitionism (desiring to rid the country of slavery by force – as opposed to the much more widespread, mainstream desire in all parts of the country for emancipation of slaves by gradual, lawful reform) increased hostile sentiments between South and North. The abolitionist movement appears also to have been exploited by Unitarian, transcendentalist intellectuals in New England, supported by men of great industrial wealth and their radical political allies in the U.S. Senate. Such senatorial leaders as Thaddeus Stevens of Pennsylvania and Charles Sumner of Massachusetts led the fragile Union to the brink of war in hopes of turning what they perceived as a too conservative, constitutional republic into a more radically liberalized modern democracy.

(Part of this half-forgotten story is intriguingly told by New York-born writer, Otto Scott, in *The Secret Six*).

The underlying issues which finally split the United States into two warring sections may – ironically – have been more clearly described by a contemporary Englishman than by any American of that time. Lord Acton highlighted these fatal issues in the momentous year of 1861 in a famous essay, 'Political Causes of the American Revolution.' He showed that the 1776 War for Independence was not an ideological 'revolution' (as was the 1789 French Revolution), whereas the War Between the States actually constituted a true revolution in terms of radically changed political theory and practice, running strongly contrary to the past.

Acton noted that the 1776 struggle concerned independence or territorial freedom, while the 1861 struggle (in the wake of the French Revolution) concerned the humanist ideal of demo-cratic egalitarianism. 'Far from being the product of a democratic revolution, and of an opposition to English institutions, the constitution of the United States [composed in the late 1780s – editor] was the result of a powerful reaction against democracy, and in favour of the traditions of the mother country.'[5]

But if the 1770s and '80s were a time of essentially conservative constitutional measures designed to insure freedom on the North American continent, by contrast, the 1850s and '60s proved to be a period of radical democratic change, motivated in part by the goal of enforcing human equality. This, in the truest sense of the word, constituted a revolution. This revolution in social and political thought had occurred among northern intellectuals and politicians, while the southern leadership continued stoutly to maintain the older view which extolled freedom over equality (if and when there was a conflict between the two values). This crucial difference was the major point at issue between the two sections of the American Republic.

Acton quotes the great South Carolina statesman, John C. Calhoun, in order to bring out the changed (or 'revolutionary') relationship of the central government in Washington to the individual states by the mid-nineteenth century. The Southerners believed that the Northerners were using their sheer majority power to circumvent the constitution, which protected the minority (the Southern states, for instance), and gave them the right to be different from popular majority opinions.

According to Calhoun:

'If the will of a majority of Congress is to be the supreme law of the land, it is clear that the constitution is a dead letter, and has utterly failed of the very object for which it was designed – the protection of the rights of the minority . . . the naked question is, whether ours is a federal or a consolidated government; a constitutional or absolute one; a government resting ultimately on the solid basis of the sovereignty of the states, or on the unrestrained will of a majority . . . in which injustice and violence and force must finally prevail.'[6]

The Unitarian intellectuals, the abolitionist media and the 'radical Republicans' in Congress laboured long and hard to move 'the will of the majority' of the North into a forced confrontation with the recalcitrant southern constitutionalist minority. And the South (especially South Carolina, as the Virginia Reformed theologian, Robert L. Dabney, once noted) had a large supply of 'hot-heads', who were too impatient with the rough and tumble of national political debate, and were all too eager to take drastic action.

Of course, the abolitionists and transcendentalist intellectuals, whatever their influence may have been, could not have brought about the war of 1861 if the conservatives of the South, guided and inspired by their own Reformed theologians, had not been so utterly unwilling to consider that there was truth in the allegations hurled against them for slave-holding. After the 1830s, the conservative theologians of the South, such as J. H. Thornwell, developed a biblical defense for slavery. Unfortunately, they did not take into serious consideration the fact that the blacks had been stolen from their homeland and that for Christians to buy stolen property is wrong.

From our late twentieth-century viewpoint, we might wish that pre-Civil War theologians had studied what, if any, were the implications of the Old Jubilee release of the captives. This issue has been addressed since the 1960s by writers from such differing viewpoints as the Liberation theologians and the Theonomists. But classical Protestantism of the nineteenth century had not even thought of, much less systematically developed, such a concept. More to the point, in terms of their own age, they were able somehow to overlook the obvious implications of the freedom and equality that we have in Jesus Christ. In a word, their reading of Scripture was hampered and twisted by the degree of fallenness which remained in their culture (as in every other culture). The United States of America and the still largely segregated churches of the land have not yet ceased to pay a price for this woeful failure. And yet, it may be easier for us twentieth-century Christians to criticize our erring forefathers for their blind spots than to see and to repent of our own.

By 1865, the South was eventually overwhelmed by the North, who outnumbered them by as much as six or seven to one. The slaves were freed, and the South was officially punished in various ways, economically and politically, for over ten gruelling, depressing years. Citizenship and the right to vote were restored in 1876. The impoverishment and persecution of the Southern states by the central government during the so-called 'Reconstruction' (1865–1876) left a bitter taste in the mouths of Southern whites both toward Northerners and in all too many cases toward Southern blacks. There were, of course, negative repercussions. The 'solid South' (i.e., the vast majority of white inhabitants including their church leadership) stood together to protect their culture. They officially segregated themselves from the freed black people until this defense was broken down by law in the 1950s and 1960s. For the most part, the Southern evangelical church failed to have a biblical vision which would have brought challenge and turmoil and then renewal and healing in this area. One is glad to testify that there have been profound and biblical changes in Southern evangelicalism in this respect since the 1950s.

But on the positive side of the debilitating, humiliating Reconstruction period, the ordinary people of the South were in a sense forced to see through the transitory and pretentious nature of material prosperity and political power, and they did have a refuge to which they could turn. Many sociologists believe that evangelical religion became even more deeply entrenched in the daily personal and institutional life of the Southern mind after the defeat of 1865 and the degradation of the 1870s. Certainly, according to Romans 5, 'tribulation works character' (at least in those who are regenerate), and it is not without significance that in the fundamentalist-modernist controversy of the 1920s and 1930s, the churches of the South stood massively with the defenders of the orthodox, biblical faith. Thus, in the period between the two world wars, the faith of the fathers was, as far as fundamentals are concerned, just as strong in most of the South as it had been in 1840 or 1740 or even 1640, though the mainline denominational seminaries and colleges were already being influenced by liberal, higher-critical thinking in many instances.

But there is more to the faith than the 'five fundamentals', which, as far as they go, did last longer in the South than elsewhere. Therefore, sound as most Southern churches may have been as late as 1930 or 1940 on such fundamental beliefs as the inspiration of Scripture and salvation through the blood atonement of Christ, the four men whom we study here would have been very saddened to see how far the Presbyterians, Baptists and Episcopalians had declined from the strong, God-centered soteriology, and world-and-life view which they had all held to a considerable extent. Instead, the churches lapsed into a broadly evangelical, man-centered type of soteriology, a lack of serious church discipline, and an all-too-frequent separation (if not dichotomy) between personal piety and business, educational and social/cultural life. Much of this decline from sound Calvinism in the Southern denominations occurred between approximately 1870 and 1930.

Since 1930 strong winds of change have swept across the South, as well as the rest of the world, and the years since 1950 have witnessed two things happening concurrently in the Southern churches: a decay of faith under the onslaught of post-Enlightenment liberalism and a renewal of faith in terms of a fervent recommitment to outreach on the basis of the biblical gospel. While much of the leadership of the mainline denominations has long since been captured by men with liberal commitments, still there has been a tremendous growth of smaller, newer, evangelical, conservative churches and, in some cases, significant renewal movements in established denominations.

Since the psalmist reminds us that our covenant-keeping

God treasures up the tears of his saints in a bottle, we may well believe that he has treasured up the prayers and tears and vision of such as Girardeau, Thornwell, Palmer and Baker for their descendants in their loved homeland. We may pray, too, that the day may dawn when the influence of these prayers and tears will be released in revival blessings upon a needy Southern people.

PART ONE

DANIEL BAKER: EVANGELISM WITH POWER

I

FROM RURAL GEORGIA TO HAMPDEN-SYDNEY AND PRINCETON

Speaking prophetically of the glad evangelical outreach of the gospel of Christ, the Old Testament prophet Isaiah exclaims: 'How beautiful upon the mountains are the feet of him that bringeth good tidings, that publisheth peace; that bringeth good tidings of good, that publisheth salvation; that saith unto Zion, Thy God reigneth!' (Isa. 52:7). These very words are taken up by the Apostle Paul, in Romans 10:15, in the context of the joyful extension of salvation in Christ to those who are lost. There could not be a better way of characterizing the effects of the life and preaching of the great Southern evangelist, Daniel Baker of Georgia, than this verse about beautiful feet hastening with glad tidings across waste places.

The tender beauty of the musical strains given this verse in the score of Handel's 'Messiah' somehow seems to capture the lovely tone that resounded from Baker's tireless, widespread ministry in the Southern and Southwestern states in the first half of the nineteenth century. If we keep in mind the two concepts which flow from the image of beautiful feet – beauty (consisting in life-changing gladness) and moving feet (which by ceaseless activity bring that gospel gladness to the needy) – we shall have isolated the keynotes of the extremely influential life of this Calvinistic evangelist.

We shall find these same keynotes consistently ringing through our consideration of his beneficial influence on pre-Confederate society, as we look at his life, the times of quickening and revival that accompanied much of his ministry, his evangelistic methodology and especially his preaching.

Daniel Baker was born on the 17th of August 1791 in Midway, Liberty County, Georgia. He was 'descended from Puritan parentage.'[1] One normally thinks of Puritans in North America as being restricted to the cold, austere climate of Massachusetts and Connecticut with their small farms, strong, literate middle class, traditional town meetings and Christopher-Wren-inspired, white-wooden Congregational churches. But in 1695 a large group of New England Puritans moved en masse to South Carolina and settled some 18 miles upriver from Charleston, which was the heartland of the old Low Country, Southern Plantation, slave-based culture. They called their new settlement Dorchester, after their home in both New England and old England. Having felt the lack of space for agricultural expansion, the entire church community of Dorchester moved in 1754 from near Charleston to a vast tract of nearly thirty-two thousand acres, granted by the Council of Georgia in Liberty County, not many miles distant from Savannah.

> A log church was immediately built, and an agreement entered into among the members. It marks the character of these pious people, that, in this agreement, in order to leave their 'children after them compactly settled together,' no member should 'sell his tract of land, or any part thereof, to any stranger or person out of the Society, without first giving the refusal of its purchase to the Society.' In 1757, a larger house of worship was completed.[2]

Here, in this wealthy, traditional Southern lowland of wide, dark-watered rivers, ancient live oaks draped in Spanish moss, old rice marshes rich with game birds, broad cotton fields worked by gangs of black slaves, and elegant plantation houses built with Georgian symmetry or later Greek-Revival verandas, the former Northern Puritans became very much an integral part of the pre-civil War Southeastern Atlantic culture. Yet they never lost (at least, not before the twentieth century) their firm Calvinistic convictions about theology and church discipline. The eighteenth- and nineteenth-century grandsons and great-grandsons who spoke with a soft, genteel Southern accent would have explained the basic meaning of life in the same words that their New English forefathers would have uttered in the more clipped cadences of their Yankee accent: 'Man's chief end is to glorify God and to enjoy him forever.'

This strong and vital Puritan Congregational church in Liberty County, Georgia, was called Midway. For all practical purposes it was Presbyterian, in that it sent literally scores of its sons into the Presbyterian ministry as preachers, missionaries and professors. The first Professor of Columbia Theological Seminary (the Presbyterian institution of the synods of South Carolina and Georgia), Thomas Goulding, was a son of Midway Church, as was the famous evangelist to the slaves, Charles C. Jones. The historian of Southern Presbyterianism, E. T. Thompson, had to devote a section of one of his three volumes to the influence of this officially Congregational church.

Daniel Baker's ancestors had been a central part of this religious community from its original movement in Devon and Dorset, England, to Massachusetts, to Dorchester, South Carolina, and to Georgia. Though his parents were not nearly so wealthy in this world's goods as, for instance, the family of Charles C. Jones, they were highly respected people. His father, William Baker, was a faithful deacon in the Midway Church, and his grandfather had suffered for his convictions during the American Revolution.

Daniel Baker, in his later years, looking back on his parents' generation at Midway Church, noted in particular these aspects of their spirituality:

> They were a race, the chief culture of whose heart, conscience, and understanding was at the family altar and in the closet; was in the Sabbath sanctuary, that central home of their souls; was in often repeated seasons of fasting and prayer, and gathered in real as well as outward brotherhood around the table of the Lord's Supper. With them religion was a matter of their brightest hopes, their warmest feelings, their deepest convictions; it was the knowledge in which their servants and children were chiefly instructed – the thing to which they instinctively and habitually subordinated everything else.[3]

Baker's mother died when he was an infant and his father died when he was only eight years old. He felt this loss of his parents deeply and continued to mention it even in his old age. Often he would visit their graves and as a child would weep, especially at the grave of his mother – over relationships he had never or at least scarcely known. He was looked after by a kindly aunt, who was a strong Christian, and also by an older sister.

As we shall see, one of the abiding characteristics of the fairly long life of Daniel Baker was a quiet and radiant happiness. A close look at his childhood, and at the turmoil of his later life, will indicate that the almost constant joy which his contemporaries noted in him could scarcely have come from easy or luxurious circumstances – either in his childhood or later. In a sermon preached during his mature years, Baker refers to one of the sad scenes of his own upbringing:

I knew once a little orphan boy, a motherless child; an elder sister, whom he loved, was displeased with him. The poor little orphan boy was much distressed, and could not be happy without being restored to his sister's love. Gathering all the little money which he had been accumulating for a long time, amounting to about fifty cents, he laid it all out for a little matter which he thought would please his sister and sent it to her as a kind of peace-offering or token of his desire to be on good terms with her. This gift was rejected. It was sent back, and contemptuously dashed upon the floor at his feet. It almost broke his heart . . . I was that little orphan boy.[4]

The source of his lifelong joy must be found outside his personal circumstances. Paradoxically, his very deprivation of father and mother seems to have been providentially blessed to him, for it left a very tender place which opened him to the love and joy of a Father's house above. Baker relates:

Sometimes I would look around, and when I saw other children who had mothers to love them and give them good things, it made me very sad to think that I had no dear mother on earth, to love me and give me good things. Sometimes I would take up the idea that no body loved me; but I thought if my mother was on earth she would love me if no body else did, but she was gone to heaven. Well, I will meet my mother there.

He then reveals that when about eight years old, he had a dream of seeing his mother among the angels. He states:

. . . and the next morning I resolved (if I could) to meet my mother in heaven – and the idea of not meeting my mother in heaven was more than I could bear.[5]

From the spiritual vantage point of his later years, Baker stated that he had been outwardly religious – but in fact, inwardly, a Pharisee – until he was around 14 years old. But the Spirit of truth did not leave him in his self-righteous slumber:

> . . . one Friday afternoon, after getting my Shorter Catechism lesson in school, I turned over towards the end of the book, and read a dialogue, in verse, between *Christ, Youth and the Devil*; this made a very great impression upon me. And my serious impressions, if I recollect right, were very much deepened by a frightful dream which I had. I thought I died suddenly, and woke up in hell! The first overwhelming thought was, that I was actually in eternity, and my day of grace was over for ever! O, I thought I would give the world if I could have only one hour more to seek salvation in! . . . I much feared that I should never meet my mother in heaven after all. I did wish that I was a bird, or insect, or any thing that had not to meet God in the judgment day![6]

Some time later, young Baker was terrified during a fierce thunderstorm, and made vows to God, but the months went on and he still felt no real peace of soul. The only real spiritual encouragement he had during this time of conviction came from a black man named Joe, who served Baker's sister Rebecca. Just when things were at their darkest, the clouds began to rift:

> After going on in darkness for many months, fearing the worst, and not knowing what to do, I took up the hymn book one day, and read the hymn beginning with these words:
>
> 'Come humble sinner, in whose breast'
>
> coming to these lines:
>
> 'But if I perish, I will pray,
> And perish only there.'
>
> My mind was made up. I went out into the grove, and resolved that if I perished, I would perish at my Savior's feet. If I did perish, I would perish praying. I went out in great distress, I returned with great joy. In prayer my mind experienced a sweet relief; I had new views of my Savior, and saw that Christ could save even so great a sinner as I was.[7]

From the time of his conversion at the age of 14, Daniel seemed to have felt the definite call to be a preacher. However, his resolve in this regard was weakened when soon afterwards he was taken out of school and sent to the large, neighboring port city of Savannah to work as a clerk in a dry-goods and grocery store. Later he was taken by a different family into the cotton brokerage business, with large prospects of success and financial and social advancement. Both of the families with which he lived in the proud and elegant city of Savannah were morally upright and very respected, but neither was evangelical at all. Young Daniel came under the influence of a worldly group of young people, so that he began to neglect the religious life and to frequent beer-gardens, though 'not without many checks of conscience.'[8]

The Spirit of truth would not leave him alone. Soon after his Christian resolves weakened, Baker noted, 'as the providence of God would have it, several things occurred to hold me in check.' Baker was nearly shot by accident while hunting, and soon thereafter, on the Sabbath day, he nearly drowned in the Savannah river while bathing. He wrote, '. . . and to crown the matter, I was taken very sick and within a few hours was brought very low, even apparently to the borders of the grave.'[9]

But these near disasters to his own life scarcely made an impression compared to his feelings on the sudden death of an unsaved young companion:

> The death was announced from the pulpit by Doctor Kollock, after preaching a very eloquent and powerful discourse. I was in church at the time, and the announcement came upon my ear as a clap of thunder from a clear sky. I had been playing cards with him a few nights before; he was then the very picture of health. And is Vanderlot dead! O, dreadful, thought I; he certainly was not prepared. And what if I had been taken![10]

These things stabbed him awake once again to the true value of the Christian life with the overwhelming eternal realities standing behind it. Braving the ridicule of his worldly friends, he plucked up courage to walk into a shop and purchase a Bible, which became his constant companion. He resolved once more to enter the preaching ministry, but at the age of nineteen was seriously hampered by his lack of education, and his lack of financial means to make up for lost time.

In the good providence of God, he received the offer of a scholarship to Hampden-Sydney College, the Presbyterian institution in Virginia, from its eminently pious president, Dr

Moses Hoge. This was accepted and it was into Hoge's home that Daniel Baker moved in the summer of 1811.

Though he felt himself somewhat intellectually disadvantaged, Baker (older than most of his classmates) worked very hard at being a good student. He found Latin grammar particularly difficult, but persisted and made good progress. While at Hampden-Sydney, he made a public profession of faith in Christ, uniting with the (Presbyterian) College Church, of which Robert L. Dabney was co-pastor many years later.

During this time Baker's spiritual life and influence greatly advanced. Somewhat like the young Jonathan Edwards, the student Baker kept a series of 'Resolutions' such as these:

Resolved, That I am too prone to indulge in improper levity in conversation; that in future I will endeavor to avoid every wicked sally of mirth or pleasantry, particularly on the Lord's day.
Resolved, That I will frequently pray to Almighty God to point out all my vices and follies, and supplicate his grace to dispose me to turn from them.[11]
Resolved, That I am not sufficiently zealous in the cause of Christ; on that account it shall be my indispensable duty frequently to pray that I may feel a more lively interest in the prosperity of Zion, that I may be inspired with a pure, ardent and unabating zeal in so glorious a cause.[12]

It was during these student years that the unfailing joy of Daniel Baker began to be noted by his fellows: his joy flowed from another world. Far from being based on superficial views of himself or of his Savior, his joy co-existed with the deepest and soberest reflection on solemn realities that frighten most people – and hence are avoided.

The eighteenth-century Scottish evangelical theologian, John Witherspoon, emigrated to America as head of New Jersey College (later Princeton University) some years before the American Revolution – which he strongly supported. His writings were of great help to Daniel Baker in taking these deep foundational views which would stand him in good stead over the long years of a demanding and fruitful ministry. Baker wrote in his diary:

Sunday. This day I finished the perusal of Witherspoon on Regeneration, a work which has afforded me peculiar delight and satisfaction. I

think I have derived much advantage from it; let it be my care to recommend it to others . . . In considering the characteristics of a regenerate person, as there, and in other works laid down, and in carefully examining my heart, I think I have experienced some saving change, have had some sweet evidences of an interest in my Savior's love. O rapturous thought! how vain, empty, and insignificant are all earthly enjoyments when compared with the enjoyments of a reconciled God and Savior. Poor wretches, who feed on the vile husks of this world, when there are such riches treasured up in Christ Jesus! O, how wonderful is it that God should have called upon me – me, so vile and ungrateful a rebel, to feed on the rich dainties of his love, while so many others have been passed by! O, it was free, sovereign, discriminating grace! . . .
Lord, may I henceforth live devoted to thee – live unreservedly to him who hath loved me and given himself for me. O Lord, I think I sincerely hate all sin, enable me for the future to resist more vigorously its assaults. I think I love thee unfeignedly; O, enable me to increase more and more. O Lord, I long to praise thee in more noble strains . . . Let me not rest with any attainments, but may I continually press forward in the divine life; may I daily become more and more assimilated to thine own glorious image, and more and more ripe for thy enjoyment hereafter.[13]

Baker's heart-humbling and soul-thrilling views of Christ in his own spiritual exercises could not fail to make an impact on his fellows. He started a fervent praying society in the college, which a number of the students joined. One particularly profane student fell under Baker's influence and was joyfully converted. Behind Baker's growing spiritual influence lay 'a life hid with Christ in God.' Concerning that period, Baker wrote in his diary:

. . . for a considerable time, (with some interruption), I seemed to bathe in the love of God, as in the sunlight of heaven. Frequently I would go out into the woods to meditate and to pray, and not infrequently, my soul being as the chariots of Amminadab, I would in my solitary walks break out into expressions of delight, and would for some considerable time go humming these and similar words, 'Victory! Glory! Alleluia!' Filled with zeal and love, I had my heart greatly drawn out towards my fellow-students. I conversed with some, I wrote to others, and invited many to come to the prayer-meetings, weekly held in the house of the President; and I believe that my efforts to do good, in various ways, were not in vain.[14]

Soon, the scenes of Baker's life were to change so that his deep, glad and compassionate nature would shed a beneficent influence on a much larger scale in Princeton College in New Jersey. Owing in part to the dislocations caused in Virginia by the war of 1812 with Great Britain, the educational opportunities offered at Hampden-Sydney were now at a low ebb. Hence, Daniel Baker moved to Princeton for the winter session of 1813, joining the junior class.

According to his own estimate, as well as the various histories of the college, 'At this time religion was at a very low ebb in the college. There were about one hundred and forty-five students, and of these, only six, so far as I knew, made any profession of religion . . .'[15] Young Daniel Baker was the instrument God used to open the way for revival in this dead, nominal situation. Baker wrote:

Feeling it my duty to do what I could for my fellow-students in Princeton, as at Hampden-Sydney College, I selected certain individuals to be made the subjects of special prayer and effort . . . I proposed to my three associates, Price, Allen, and Biggs, that we should establish a weekly prayer-meeting for the especial purpose of praying for a revival of religion in College . . . We went from room to room, conversing on the subject of religion only.[16]

Before long, these students were divinely blessed. Two profound judges of Christian experience, Dr Ashbel Green (President of Princeton, and later leader of the 'Old School' forces in the American Presbyterian Church) and Professor Archibald Alexander (first Professor of Princeton Seminary and teacher of Charles Hodge) deemed these blessed times to be a genuine revival of religion in Nassau Hall College (i.e. Princeton).

Baker wrote at the time:

O, it was a beautiful sight to see some seventy or eighty young men under the influence of deep religious feeling, about forty-five of whom were rejoicing in Christ. It was worth an angel's visit from the skies, to see them walking, so lovingly, arm in arm, or in groups, talking about the great things the Lord had done for them.[17]

This quickening movement, like any genuine revival, bore lasting fruit in the kingdom of God. Among the students who were subjects of this work of the Spirit:

. . . some forty-five or fifty, were, in the judgment of charity, soundly converted. About twenty or thirty, I should think, became ministers of the gospel, several of whom became pillars of the Church; two at the present time are distinguished bishops of the Episcopal Church; one has been, and perhaps still is, president of a College, another [Hodge], according to a British print, is 'the greatest divine now living,' whilst another has become famous as a missionary to the Sandwich Islands . . .[18]

Thus, the class which graduated from Princeton in 1815 included an unusually large percentage of highly qualified Christian leaders, who would make their mark for the gospel all across the world in years to come. Daniel Baker was not the least among that Spirit-filled band. His humble and glad piety, and his determination to do all that he could to introduce others to the joy which he knew in Christ, were already in evidence as characteristics which would mark his pilgrimage to the very end.

Many years later, one of his Princeton classmates described the impression Baker made:

Besides the usual promise of fair talents, untiring industry, and great steadfastness of purpose in doing good, there was about this man a singular sweetness of disposition and loving character of his piety (loving, we mean in spirit like that of Rutherford's letters and Solomon's Songs, not, of course, in language), and these marked the man, and continued, I believe, more or less throughout life.[19]

2

FIRST PASTORATES

Although Baker had originally intended to return to Princeton in order to enter the seminary, several of his friends prevailed on him not to do so, but instead to take his theological training under the Rev. William Hill, pastor of the Presbyterian church in Winchester, Virginia, and the authorized teacher of theological students under the care of his presbytery. We are not sure why he was urged to return to Virginia, but possibly it may have been to make it more likely that his talents would be reserved for the Southern states with their rapidly expanding population towards the Southwest.

William Hill, good man though he was, does not appear to have taken his duties as theological master very seriously, for he was absent much of the time on preaching tours, leaving his young student in charge of the duties of his parish. Baker later would write:

> Mr. Hill had strangely neglected my theological studies, and so far as I can now recollect, had put no book in my hand save *Butler's Analogy*. I, however, made great use of the Shorter Catechism; I was told that it was an admirable 'summary,' and I studied that and my Bible.[20]

Indeed, his higher theological training had been so neglected, that when it came time for his ordination, the presbytery debated long and hard over whether or not he was ready to take up the work of the ministry. It was, however, decided to ordain him and when he delivered his 'popular discourse' from Ephesians 2:8, many were moved to tears. Baker immediately, with the blessing of the presbytery, moved into widespread preaching tours in that region of Virginia. Many were converted, and Baker himself stated, 'I was astonished, and marveled that my few sermons should be so remarkably blessed.'[21] He wrote this prayer the week before he was licensed by presbytery:

To thee, O my God, do I commit myself, and again would I solemnly renew the dedication of myself and my all to thy service. O condescend to accept the unworthy offering, and lay me out for thy glory. I ask not to be rich in silver and gold, and to be admired and caressed; I ask to be rich in faith and good works, and to be blessed and owned in my labours of love. I ask not to be exempted from grievous trials and persecutions, but I ask grace to glorify thee in the hour of trial; grace to be useful, grace to be triumphant in death, and grace to reach, at length, the Mount Zion above, where I may for ever sing the triumphs of my dearest Lord. To thee, O my God, do I now commit my way; be pleased to direct my paths, for the Redeemer's sake. Amen.[22]

We have mentioned earlier that radiant joy was characteristic of Daniel Baker from his time at Hampden-Sydney College to the close of his earthly career, and that this quiet happiness seems to have had a contagious influence on those around him. His son, William Baker, who wrote his biography, stated that his father's remarkably steady cheer was made the easier – from the human perspective – by his excellent health, strong constitution, untiring energy, and almost unlimited capacity for labor. According to William, 'Avoiding all stimulants, with a healthful appetite for food, careless of its quality – all that he required was a certain amount of sleep.'[23]

Owing to his health, his cheerfulness also was never impaired; in fact, amounted, all the year around, to steady joyousness. No one, in or out of his family, can remember even a momentary cloud of depression on his sunny brow, or a breath of petulance on his smiling lips. He may have been angry at times, but never for an instant cross.[24]

And yet, good health and naturally energetic 'animal spirits', while helpful in maintaining his radiant temperament, are far from the ultimate explanation of it. His son isolates the real source of this treasure which no money can buy:

There is a joy which lends a deeper glow to the cheek, and a brighter sparkle to the eye, and a sweeter song to the lips, even of the angels in the presence of God – the joy over a repenting sinner. Of this celestial joy, the subject of this memoir had a full share – a larger share, perhaps, than generally falls to those on this side the gates of heaven. It need scarce be said, his energy, cheerfulness, buoyancy, had their fountain-head in his faith in God, manifested in Christ; but their deep, wide, unobstructed channels were in his healthfulness of body.[25]

Although Daniel Baker seems to have derived all too little theological benefit from his time under the tutelage of William Hill, by his presence in that locality he did get one of the greatest blessings of his life, a loving and faithful wife, Elizabeth McRobert. She was the daughter of the distinguished lawyer, Theodoric McRobert, and granddaughter of the well-known Presbyterian minister, Rev. Archibald McRobert, a Scottish emigrant. He was married to this lady of piety and kindness for forty-two years. She bore him several children, and faithfully stood with him through the difficulties of his long, itinerant missionary existence (at some emotional cost to herself, as we see from his letters to her). She outlived him only by a few months.

For over a year after his marriage in 1816, Baker undertook itinerant preaching at various places in Virginia and then in his home territory in Georgia. There were consistently large crowds and apparently numerous converts, including a number of openly profane persons. In 1818, he accepted the pastorate of the United Congregations of Harrisonburg and New Erection in Rockingham County, Virginia. To supplement his income, he also taught school there for about two years. When he left this charge about 1821, one of his elders could say to him, 'Mr. Baker, you have endeared yourself to the hearts of the people.'[26] The churches were blessed under his labors and members were added, but his heart seemed to have been set upon a traveling ministry. During a missionary tour in Western Virginia (an area of growing population and relatively few gospel privileges), the glad responsiveness of the scattered settlers exercised a strong pull upon him and he wrote, 'I began to have a hankering after a missionary life . . .'[27]

An appendix to Baker's *Revival Sermons: Second Series* may give us some insight into the Samson-like strength of the call that seemed to pull him into missionary preaching in remote

Southern and Southwestern areas. He gives this account of an incident that seems to have lastingly touched his heart and marked his life:

Having been sent an appointment to preach one sermon in a certain place, on a week day, I rode up at the hour appointed, and was astonished to see so many horses hitched all around. As no house near at hand could accommodate the persons assembled, we went into the grove, and had such accommodations as we could get. I preached a long sermon, and every individual seemed to listen with an eagerness which I had rarely ever witnessed before. On singing the last hymn, I rose, and gave them some parting words. I then pronounced the blessing, but was not permitted to go; and consented to preach another sermon, after a short recess.[28]

Baker goes on to relate that after he had preached the second sermon, the large, grateful crowd refused to leave and begged for another sermon. He then preached a third sermon (this one of only twenty minutes in length), and though the sun was by now setting, the eager people still declined to disperse:

Hearts were melting, and tears were in many eyes! They must still have 'some more words'. I began again to speak, and had not continued long, when (my face being turned to the West) I saw a dark cloud rising. It began to lighten, it began to thunder, but none save myself seemed to know that the storm was near. At length, rain drops began to descend. 'Friends,' said I, 'a storm is at hand; we had better retire.' Then, and not until then, did they leave their seats in the grove: and one man, Captain Wright, coming to me, grasped my hand with much emotion, and tears running down his cheeks, said, 'Stranger, for God's sake come back, or send some one to preach to us the gospel.'[29]

After resigning his first pastorate, Baker attended the General Assembly of the Presbyterian Church in Philadelphia (1821). On his way back to Virginia, he preached for several weeks in Washington, D.C., but had to hasten home to Prince Edward, Virginia, because of the death of his second son, Daniel Speece. He then went to his home territory in Georgia and preached in several places, including the large and important Independent Presbyterian Church of Savannah. Consequently he was given a call both to the great church in Savannah and to the small Second Presbyterian Church in

Washington. Declining the far more prestigious position and much larger salary, Baker accepted the call to the small charge in Washington. In fact, the salary was so small in Washington that he had to be a 'tentmaker' once again, serving a clerkship in the Land Office in addition to his ministerial duties.

He served this church until 1828, and though there was no revival such as he had seen in his student days or later experience, he stated, '. . . we had what may be called heavenly dew'.[30] The number of communicants within the church increased considerably. But the faithful and zealous pastor was not content to see the gospel message confined within the walls of their church building:

> During one season, besides preaching three times in the church on the Sabbath, I preached in the afternoon in the market-house, on Pennsylvania Avenue, to a mixed multitude of loafers, loungers, the sons of the bottle, and the sons of Ham. I hope much good was done by this act of obedience to the command, 'Go out into the streets and lanes of the city and compel them to come in.'[31]

Daniel Baker appears to have made a strong impact on Washington during his stay of approximately six years. John Quincy Adams and General Andrew Jackson regularly attended his preaching and, in later years, signed a call urging him to return to the capital. But this sort of fame in no sense turned Baker's head. Then, as in later years, when he was used by God to bring many élite members of society to salvation through the faithful preaching of Christ, the result was a deeper humility and a greater joy in Christ, 'whom not having seen, he loved.'

A respected member of the Baptist Church, who lived in Washington during these years of Baker's ministry, described it as follows:

> . . . I frequently attended at his place of worship. I preferred his ministry, not because it was the most intellectual, but because it was spiritual, fervent, and enforced by a consistent life. He was a man of prayer; he preached to save souls; he walked with God. He was sincere, earnest, simple-minded. He did one thing, and did it well.[32]

Baker did more than preach in Washington; he wrote an excellent book entitled, *A Scriptural View of Baptism*, which, in my view, should be reprinted today. Although he was, as we have seen, lacking in technical theological training, this volume shows that he had a sound and insightful theological instinct both for the major patterns of covenantal theology as well as for controverted details concerning the baptism of the infants of believers. It is written in an unusually clear and attractive English style, and manifests a charitable spirit towards Christian brothers who take a different line on the subject. Indeed, this clarity of style and charity of spirit consistently also marked Baker's preaching and personal dealings. Such a frame of mind meant that he would be well prepared for the larger tasks that lay open before him on the national and interdenominational scale.

In many ways, the little church in Washington was always Baker's first love. Eventually though, and not without an emotional struggle, he came to believe that he must accept a further call to the pastorate of the Independent Presbyterian Church in Savannah, where he had once regularly attended in his early teens. This socially distinguished church had a pre-eminent position in the important port of Savannah. Its impressive building, which still stands just as it was in Baker's day, was said to have been modeled on St Martin-in-the-Fields of London – though the Savannah church is in fact considerably larger than its inspiration in London.

The famous New York literary critic and novelist, William Dean Howells, writing with unrestrained enthusiasm in *Harper's Magazine*, described this church as it looked in 1919 (it was no different then, or today than it was in Baker's time): 'The structure on the outside is of such Sir Christopher Wrennish renaissance that one might seem to be looking at it in a London street; but the interior is of such unique loveliness that no church in London may compare with it. Whoever would realize its beauty must go at once to Savannah and forget for one beatific moment in its presence the ceilings of Tiepolo and the roofs of Veronese.'[33]

Lowell Mason, author of such hymn tunes as 'From Greenland's Icy Mountains' and the American tune of 'When I Survey the Wondrous Cross,' was for some years its organist. One of Baker's near successors in the pastorate of this church, Dr I. K. Axson, who preached there for several decades in the late nineteenth century, was the maternal grandfather of Woodrow Wilson, President of the United States in the years around World War I.[34]

To this imposing church, which, in the words of Baker in a letter to the members of his old church in Washington, 'embraces a great portion of the wealth and intelligence of the city,'[35] he came as a humble but determined advocate of the cross in 1828. Apparently, he soon realized that his task there would not be an easy one. The congregation was in a divided condition. In addition there seems to have been a lethargy in its midst with a measure of smugness and a 'resting upon past laurels,' not to mention a temptation to elements of pride in social distinctions.[36] And yet at the same time, Baker noted that there was a beautiful tenderness and openness of spirit toward the things of God among many – including leading elders – in this large congregation.[37] Thus, despite the difficulties, he found strong spiritual and personal support from the start of his ministry, and he felt encouraged to seek God's best for these people.

Although he preached fearlessly for many months, he had to write in the August of 1830:

> . . . Not satisfied either with myself or the state of things in the church, I took *Payson's Memoirs* in my hand, and going out early that morning, I spent nearly the whole day in a distant graveyard, engaged in reading and fasting and prayer. That day marks a memorable era in the history of my life. Returning to my dwelling that evening, about the setting of the sun, I resolved, by the grace of God, to turn over a new leaf, and in preaching and pastoral visitations to be more faithful and diligent than I had ever been.[38]

More specifically, Daniel Baker went on to state that the reading of *Payson's Memoirs* (minister of Portland, Maine) brought a quickening into his own spirit, which helped him realize some uncomfortable facts about his own condition:

> O, what a dead state have I been in for a length of time, and how unblessed my labors! I know not that a single individual has been awakened under my preaching for six months past. It will not do to live on at this poor dying rate. Lord, revive me, all my help must come from thee![39]

On the evening of this same day of personal repentance and quickening in the lonely graveyard, Baker had to lead a communicants' class. There was a new spirit abroad in this meeting – of tenderness, humility, openness and an impinging sense of eternal reality. From that time on, something different seemed to be happening in all the services of the church. Baker wrote this in his diary on the following Sabbath:

This day had something of the spirit of devotion; had liberty in praying for assistance and a blessing in preaching; preached in the morning from Ezekiel 3:17–19; had more liberty than I have had for a long time; wept myself and had the satisfaction of seeing others weep. In the afternoon preached from Isaiah 55:12, 13; at night had a solemn meeting in the Sabbath-school room; gave notice then that there would be a special prayer meeting on Tuesday evening next; and after stating the special object, invited all who felt disposed, to send in notes; told them that a box would be placed on the table, and the room opened on Monday evening to receive the notes which might be sent in.

August 17th. Had a great many at the meeting; forty-six notes were sent in and read; some were from parents, entreating that prayers might be made for their dear unconverted children . . . one from 'A sinner who desires the prayers of God's people for the conversion of his soul'; . . . some were from professors who seemed to fear that they were not on a good foundation, and some from members who felt that they were in a cold, dead state, and longed for quickening influences. I put in a note myself, requesting the prayers of my people for me; that the Lord would give me a more intense love for souls . . . and would cause me to have a richer and sweeter experience of the grace of God in my own heart.[40]

Strong signs of new life were manifesting themselves in both minister and congregation. But, as is usual in true revivals, there was opposition from within the body of the church. The form it took in Savannah was resentment against Baker's increased liberty in preaching. This will best be explained in his own words:

At this time my preaching became so plain and pointed that some persons took offense. One elder remarked that certain things which I had said from this text, 'Gray hairs are here and there, and he knoweth it not,' were unwarrantable; and another elder said to my face, 'Mr. Baker, if you continue to preach in this way, none of the young people will join our church'. 'I do not wish them to join,' said I, 'unless they are converted.'[41]

Soon afterwards, Baker convinced the session of the church to hold a special series of meetings with an outside preacher. They selected a Mr Joyce to preach, and the Holy Spirit's blessing seemed to have been upon this series, and especially upon all the corporate praying connected with it. Prayer was held in the church at sunrise, then there was preaching three times a day. These meetings lasted for only five days but during those days there was a deep, chastening impression of the presence and holiness of the Spirit of God, and some twenty persons professed conversion. But what happened after the brief meeting was undoubtedly of greater importance. Neighborhood prayer meetings were organized and met once or twice each week for many months. Other churches and denominations as well as the Independent Presbyterian began to feel the effects of the coming down of the Spirit of grace and supplication. Baker says:

This religious interest continued, without much abatement, for about one year, during which period about one hundred persons were added to the communion of my church; and the blessed work of grace extending to other churches, the whole number brought in, if I mistake not, was about two hundred and fifty.[42]

Baker had the joy of seeing the conversion of some of those leaders in the church who had opposed him most strongly. This quickening in Savannah seems to have opened the way for Baker to return once more to the life he came to like best: that of a traveling evangelist.

News of the revival in Savannah spread abroad quickly, and many churches in that part of Georgia and more especially in nearby 'Low Country' South Carolina decided to have what were then called 'protracted meetings' in hopes of getting some measure of revival blessing. Baker was of course eagerly sought after to preach at these protracted meetings. We must carefully note here that, unlike the widespread custom that has prevailed since the 1920s in the American South, of terming a yearly series of evangelistic meetings a 'revival', the Christians of Baker's time were far more careful and biblical in their terminology. They simply called these meetings 'protracted' (i.e. drawn out), unless, in fact, there was an evident quickening work of the Holy Spirit bringing profound changes in individual and community life. Then in retrospect, the meeting would be referred to as a revival. Presbyterians (and for that matter, probably the majority of other evangelical Protestants) in the nineteenth-century South clearly understood that revival was the sovereign gift of the Spirit. It could not be 'planned and administered' by the church or anyone but God. And yet in terms of Luke 11:13, the Holy Spirit is to be given in answer to prayer and thus true revival can legitimately be sought, whether in private, in regular stated services or in special meetings. And it was in the latter – special meetings – that revival was sought for in Carolina and Georgia after the quickening in Savannah of 1830–31.

The revival in Savannah and especially those revivals soon to follow in various locations of nearby Low Country, South Carolina, set the tone for the rest of Baker's fruitful and far-ranging ministry. The blessings of the Spirit upon the people and their glad responsiveness to his roving ministrations in various locations appear to have engendered in him what could perhaps be interpreted as a kind of 'divine discontent' with any settled parish ministry for the rest of his life. From 1831 to the end of his life in 1857, his ministerial activity would be an interweaving of fairly short pastorates with much longer evangelistic tours. This pattern was in full operation immediately after the Savannah awakening.

Revival broke out in three South Carolina towns where Baker labored in preaching services in 1831: Gillisonville, Beaufort and Grahamsville. At this stage, Baker was still pastor at Savannah. Interestingly, the most powerful of these revivals was deemed to have occurred in the lovely old port of Beaufort (which still preserves much of its antebellum Georgian and Federal-style architecture); a town which at that time had no Presbyterian church. Here Baker gladly alternated his preaching in the Episcopal and Baptist churches, with strong support from the ministry of both denominations. Meetings were held three times a day; the churches were packed, and there was 'a concert of prayer' at sundown each day. It is said that a considerable percentage of the population of the town was converted during this time. One of the converts was 86 years old: Colonel Daniel Stevens, who had heard George Whitefield preach. Unmoved by the sermons of the great British evangelist, he had spent his life in Unitarianism. Stephen Elliott, who later became Episcopal Bishop of Georgia, was converted, as was R. Barnwell, who became President of the University of South Carolina.

The editor of the *Beaufort Gazette* described the evident effects of the revival:

Politics were forgotten; business stood still; the shops and stores were shut; the schools closed; one subject only appeared to occupy all minds and engross all hearts. The church was filled to overflowing; . . . When the solemn stillness was broken by the voice of the preacher, citing the impenitent to appear before the judgement-seat of heaven; reproving, persuading, imploring . . . and when crowds moved forward and fell prostrate at the foot of the altar, and the rich music of hundreds of voices, and the solemn accents of prayer rose over the kneeling multitude, it was not in human hearts to resist the influence that awoke its sympathies, and spoke its purest and most elevated feeling.
Animosities long continued, were sacrificed; coldness and formality were forgotten. Our community seemed like one great family . . .[43]

The Episcopal minister there said this:

The effects of the revival were as visible upon the community as upon the church. It seasoned with its holy savor all the intercourse of society. The truths of God's word . . . were frequent themes of conversation . . . Family prayer was established in almost every house, and as you walked along the streets, in the stillness of a summer morning you might hear the united voice of each household ascending in well known hymns of praise, to the honor of their great Redeemer.
Such was the pervading influence of the religious principle upon the whole aspect of society, that it cast it into the gospel mold and stamped it with its own holy features . . . For twenty years past there has been a higher moral and religious tone, and a more intelligent and consistent profession of Christianity maintained in that little town than in any other which the writer has visited in Europe or America.[44]

3

A LIFE OF TRAVEL

Not long after the revivals of 1830–31, Baker left the largest and most influential church he would ever pastor for a less certain existence as a traveling missionary/evangelist. His salary would be reduced from two thousand dollars a year to six hundred, and he had a considerable family to support. Later, he could look back and see that the Lord never failed to provide for all his family's needs. These next few years of evangelistic tours in the old Southeast (especially South Carolina, Georgia, Alabama and Florida) he was to describe as 'the best period of my life; my labors were more abundant, and my success far beyond my most sanguine anticipations.'[45]

In these Southern states where Freemasonry has had deep and extensive influence throughout society, one of the beneficial results of Baker's missionary tours was to challenge and undercut the insidious 'righteousness by good works' viewpoint which Freemasonry had fostered almost unwittingly among much of the male population. What the Rev. Edward Palmer said about some of the churches which were touched by Baker's ministry in South Carolina could have justly been said about many others in the South:

> . . . these churches were nearly all, in the language of one of their eminent laymen, 'little better than Masonic lodges.' They had the form of godliness, but were destitute of its power. The frequenters of the race-course and the theatre found their places at the communion table. The duelist was not excluded.[46]

Palmer then relates the glorious difference made by the

outpouring of the Holy Spirit during the ministrations of Baker in these churches. Baker spent three years in these missionary tours in the Southeastern states, and many of these tours were characterized by local revivals which left effects on the community for decades to come.

Though Daniel Baker was glad to influence his native South, he was a man with a larger vision for the whole developing country. In this more national vision, Baker was different from John L. Girardeau, who would never have considered leaving the South. Of course, in Baker's time in the 1830s, feelings of animosity between North and South were not nearly so strong as they were in Girardeau's younger days in the 1850s and 60s, when his lifelong attitudes were set.

Unlike all too many Presbyterians and Episcopalians, and more like the Methodists and Baptists, Baker had his keen eye fixed on the movements of population in the still young American Republic. It was a generally recognized fact that in the 1830s there was a large stream of population leaving the old Southern seaboard for Ohio and Indiana, and in the next decade there was a similar movement towards Texas in the Southwest. Baker was to follow both of these movements in an endeavor to minister to these people who would in many cases be without regular gospel privileges. His work in Texas was to be far more significant than his brief time in the more culturally-strange Ohio.

When Baker and his family left the South to move to Ohio, his wagon broke down near Charlotte Court House, Virginia. While there, he was invited to preach. There was such a good response to his preaching that consequently he settled down in Virginia for over a year in order to hold meetings all around. It is believed that more than a thousand Virginians were converted during this year of itinerant preaching. Hence Baker rightly felt that the breaking of the shaft of his wagon was the providential hand of God, and that 'surely there is no such thing as chance.'[47]

He did eventually move to Ohio, where he held many meetings that resulted in a considerable number of conversions, but his time there was not more than a few months. He soon longed to return to his native South. This may have been related to the fervent abolitionist movement which was already stirring much of Ohio with sentiments thoroughly opposed to Southern convictions on constitutional limitations on the powers of the central government, especially as this related to economic tariffs and social policies such as slavery. Baker, unlike Dabney, Girardeau, Thornwell and Palmer, seems to have had very little interest in political and economic questions, but as a Southerner in Ohio, he could not avoid being drawn into controversial conversations. Since this ran against his nature, we can safely assume that this contributed to his leaving after such a short time.

From Ohio he went to the border state of Kentucky, where he labored as a missionary for some months until he was called to be minister of the Presbyterian church in Frankfort, Kentucky. During this transition from Ohio to Kentucky, Baker, happy man that he so regularly was, seemed to have reached perhaps a low point. E. Gildersleeve, an old South Carolinian friend of his, wrote this article in the *Charleston Observer* (Oct. 11, 1834) following a letter he had received from Baker:

> . . . this brother [Baker] . . . speaks of himself as an exile, and as forgotten by those whom he has most loved. From the strain of his communication it would appear, that his numerous epistles written to his friends in this State, in Georgia, and in Virginia, have either none of them been answered, or that the answers have failed to reach him . . . it would appear from the following extract, that he has been of late disappointed in his expectations, and feels again inclined to resume the pastoral office.[48]

The situation for Baker was more congenial in Kentucky than in Ohio, although here, as well, he did not know the height of blessing that had attended his earlier labors in the deep Southern states, or that would later be manifested in Texas. The church in Frankfort grew during the two years of his ministry, but did not experience anything close to revival. However, during this time, Baker continued making preaching tours to outlying areas and served as chaplain of the penitentiary, where he saw a number of conversions. But the church was very irregular in paying his small salary, and Baker left, under some discouragement, in 1836 for Tuscaloosa, Alabama.

Tuscaloosa and the surrounding area was to prove a place of larger blessing, but Baker had more tests to pass through before this blessing would become evident. He reached Tuscaloosa the very year that the troubles between the theological liberals and the traditional conservative Calvinists of the Presbyterian Church in the United States of America (better known as 'New School' and 'Old School') reached a peak. The controversies at the General Assembly resulted in disruption and final division of the large denomination the following year. Whereas most churches in the Southern states tended to be 'Old School', a number of Southerners – including some in Tuscaloosa (the site of the University of Alabama) – did sympathize with the New School. Thus Baker came to a congregation which was of divided opinion on this important matter.

At first Baker was like some of the leading professors of Princeton and tended to take a middle position, hoping a split could be avoided. But as the heterodoxy of the leading New School thinkers increasingly came to light, Baker took his stand on the Old School side. All of his session were with him, but there was a New School party among some of his congregation. He states in his memoirs:

> It required much prudence and much effort, on my part, to keep them from separating, and splitting the church in two; but with God's blessing, peace and quietness were finally restored; and when two General Assemblies were formed, the church of which I was pastor gave in its adhesion to the Old-School General Assembly.[49]

Baker stayed in Tuscaloosa until 1839. The church grew by 81 members, which was a good number considering the high membership standards he required and the relatively small population. He did much gospel work among the blacks of the area, as well as making periodic preaching visits to other areas. Finally the old desire to give himself full-time to missionary evangelism took hold of him afresh. At this time he wrote to a Rev. Galloway:

> . . . I am in many respects pleasantly situated here, but my field of usefulness is not as large as I could wish it, and I am kept in a very unpleasant state on account of my salary not being promptly paid – about one thousand dollars due to me at the present time. We do not preach for money, and yet without it we cannot support our families, nor pay our debts.[50]

Just at the very time that Baker was feeling inclined to leave his settled pastorate for the missionary life, he had a meeting with the well-known churchman of Kentucky, Dr John Breckinridge, whose advice was to set Baker's course for the remainder of his life. Baker wrote:

I think it was in the year 1838 that my attention was first drawn to Texas. The Rev. John Breckinridge had just visited this new republic, and upon his return, was anxious that Presbyterians should make some special efforts to send missionaries and plant churches of our faith and order in that new field . . . He gave a glowing account of Texas as an unusually promising field for missionary enterprise; and as he closed, he turned to me and said, 'Brother Baker, you are the man for Texas.'[51]

Baker then asked presbytery to dissolve his pastoral relationship with his church and to send him to Texas as the missionary of Tuscaloosa Presbytery, and salaried by them. This was agreed on by presbytery. In a real sense, this action marks the beginning of the final stage of his ministerial life, which lasted until his death in late 1857. Thus for almost two more decades, this abounding servant of God would focus his energies on the burgeoning state of Texas and on the growing population of Mississippi.

Without going into the details of his massive preaching activities there and elsewhere, we may get the flavor and recognize the broad scope of his richly blessed ministry to the old Southwest by isolating a few of the typical events that occurred during this last stage of his life. Essentially the rest of his ministry consisted of three large, long, influential tours of Texas, interspersed with brief pastorates and further missions back in the states East of the Mississippi River.

In this latter stage of Baker's ministry, something of the atmosphere of the Low Country revival years of 1831–32 seemed to have returned in many of the scenes of his labor, although his biography leaves the impression that the outpouring of the Spirit was not in the same measure or intensity as previously. Nevertheless, it is clear that his last few years in and around Texas were a time of much greater blessing than what he had known from about 1833 to 1839. But what is outstanding in the latter part of his ministerial labors is his self-denying

– and, indeed, *happy* – constancy and persistency in ceaselessly and energetically traveling, praying, preaching and visiting in both settled and remote areas. His efforts were consistently rewarded with substantial numbers of conversions – from slaves to the most powerful and influential leaders of South-western society and politics. If his previous six years had been often clouded, his last nineteen were to be, on the whole, full of sunshine in the Lord's work.

His first tour in Texas was very encouraging. He administered the first Protestant Lord's Supper on Galveston Island in 1840. He traveled widely in East Texas, preaching constantly, and often journeying and sleeping in difficult and dangerous conditions. He came down with the fever at one stage of the journey, almost sank in a leaky boat at another, and was lost at night knee-deep in a marsh at still another. By the mercies of the Lord, he not only survived but prospered – physically and spiritually. The people of Texas were generally responsive, and he saw the transformation of hundreds of lives. For the rest of his life, his heart would be knit to this frontier place.

At the end of this tour, which was more than a year's duration, he was missing his family and his family was missing him. It was particularly difficult for his wife to be separated for such long periods of time, as his letters to her demonstrate. It seemed best for the family that Baker should take a pastoral charge so that they could be together for a good while. Hence he accepted a call to be minister in Holly Springs, Mississippi. The church there was very small and the manse literally a log cabin (a glaring contrast with the elegant manse in Savannah), but in the words of Baker:

> I had a home at last; and, humble as it was, it was to me like a little palace! My labors were blessed as a pastor, and enjoying the affections, as I believed, of the people of my charge, I was a happy man.[52]

Undoubtedly part of his pleasure at being in Holly Springs for nine years (by far his longest pastorate) lay in the freedom he had to continue many preaching tours in the Mississippi territory. This area was constantly receiving new streams of settlers from the upper Southern states in the wake of peace with the Indians and the opening up of rich new lands for farming and grazing. He preached in places such as Jackson (before Governor Brown), Brandon, Vicksburg, Lexington, Canton and Yazoo City. Interestingly, in Yazoo City he stated that he had a good audience, but 'little or no liberty in consequence of echo.'[53]

Holly Springs itself experienced at least two times of quickening during these years: once under Baker's preaching and then under the preaching of the Rev. Vancourt. During one of these times of blessing, some two hundred people in this small village professed conversion, among them Daniel Baker's youngest son, who decided to go to Princeton to study for the ministry. This meant that now Baker actually had two sons in ministerial preparation at Princeton.

In a typical letter to one of his Princeton sons, the happy-spirited father wrote these words, which reveal much about his own genial religious character:

> Be sure you never omit the devotions of the closet, nor suffer yourself to pass them over in a formal and hurried manner. See to it, my son, that you enjoy religion, and enjoy it every day. On the very ground where you now are, your father had much religious enjoyment nearly thirty years ago . . .[54]

In 1848, a spirit of restlessness, perhaps part of the divine discontent with a life settled in one place, came strongly upon Daniel Baker, and once again his heart turned towards Texas. His pastorate in Holly Springs had been a happy one, and he left under the best of conditions with his people longing for him to stay. Thus he began his second tour of Texas in the June of 1848. His name was becoming well known in Texas by this time. Wherever he went, large crowds generally attended his preaching and often he would write, 'an overflowing house and great solemnity'.[55]

Even though he was now fifty-seven years old (comparatively speaking, a greater age in 1848 than in the late twentieth-century) and had to pass through wild territory, sometimes inhabited by hostile Indians, he experienced a new lease on life during this demanding second Texas tour. In a letter dated June 26, 1848, he wrote to his wife:

> O, it is pleasant to preach to a people who seem to be so eager to hear the word of life. It rouses me delightfully, and I feel as if I was in my

own native element; or as the saying is, like a fish in water. I do believe I was cut out for a missionary – no mistake. Addressing a new and hungry congregation, I seem to have new life infused into my soul. I do hope my Master has something important for me to do in Texas.[56]

During this far-ranging tour, a false report was spread in the Eastern papers that Dr Baker had been killed and scalped by Indians, and Baker wryly commented that he had the pleasure of reading his own obituary! Once, while traveling from Victoria to Wharton, Baker got lost at night in the wilds of Colorado. He decided to lie down on the prairie and sleep but was soon surrounded by the cries of wolves and panthers. So he stayed up all night protecting himself with fire. His gospel cheer and good common sense enabled him to go through many such experiences with equanimity.

Once he arrived at a Texas preaching appointment when rain was pouring in torrents. The discouraged host pastor was very apologetic about the weather. A fellow minister relates Baker's reponse:

With a tranquil smile which I shall never forget, he replied, as he laid his hand on my shoulder, 'My dear brother, the clouds are in good hands; let the clouds alone.'[57]

The minister adds that the clouds were indeed 'in good hands,' for some forty persons were brought in during the meeting, notwithstanding the rain. According to Baker's son:

. . . his belief was clear and constant that the finger of God was in every event, from the greatest down to the very least. This was the secret of his unbroken cheerfulness under the most mysterious and otherwise discouraging providences.[58]

As Baker came to the end of his fruitful second missionary tour in Texas, he had a definite vision of the growing political and social importance of the West and of its great need for Christian ministry. He saw that the established churches in the East were too slow to send out ministers. Baker was an obvious exception to the old saying that the Baptists went to the West on foot, the Methodists on horseback, while the Presbyterians and Episcopalians waited for the construction of railroads in order to travel first-class! There is some truth in this proverb, however, for while the Presbyterian, Congregational and

Episcopal churches were massively preponderant from the early settlements of the thirteen original colonies down to the 1830s, after that time they lost much of their missionary impetus within the country. The latter part of the nineteenth century reveals that they were greatly outnumbered by the Baptists and Methodists, who, like Baker, were eager to go where the people were migrating, regardless of conditions. Of course, it is only fair to add that established views concerning high educational standards for ministers made it more difficult for the older denominations. However, lack of vision would appear to have been a more serious problem than that. Baker once wrote, 'Let inferior preachers be retained in the East; let talented ones be sent to the West.'[59] But he does not seem to have been seriously heeded by his own denomination.

Baker was a good strategic thinker; he could see the long term as well as the short, and was – in this respect – like Robert L. Dabney, who thirty years after Baker's death would come to Texas in his old age and 'see visions and dream dreams' for future kingdom expansion. Both of these men (though thirty years apart in time) grasped the great need of Texas to establish its own ministerial training in light of the hesitation of Eastern theological students to come to a difficult place while there were many vacant pulpits in their own established home territory. In the 1880s Dabney was to help in the founding of the University of Texas and of Austin Theological Seminary. But as early as the 1840s Baker realized that a good Presbyterian college needed to be established in order to train the future leadership for Texas and especially ministerial leadership. Baker was to give the rest of his ministerial labors to raise funds for the founding of what would be known as Austin College. With this great goal in mind, he returned to Mississippi in order to complete his affairs, get his family, request commissioning as permanent missionary to Texas of the Presbyterian Synod so that he could return to Texas for his third, and final, tour.

According to William Benchoff, a Baptist minister of Texas, who wrote a master's thesis on the life of Baker in 1954:

> Unlike the feeling of a Kentuckian or a Virginian for their own state, the Texan has a certain defined feeling, as a nation itself, due perhaps, to its comparative size and past history. They do not regard Texas merely as a State. Dr. Baker also partook of this feeling, and the feeling grew as he

saw the population of the State increase from one hundred thousand to more than six hundred thousand.[60]

This final stage of Baker's life as a missionary to Texas would last from 1850 to his death seven years later. His goals, as we have seen, were clearly defined by this time. While he still intended to win souls and establish churches through tours of protracted meetings, he specifically hoped at the same time to collect offerings to fund Austin College. To that end, in addition to being an official Presbyterian missionary to Texas, he was appointed Permanent General Agent for the college in the April of 1850 with a regular salary. The college had been approved by presbytery and chartered under the authority of Governor Wood the year before.

After some itineration in Texas in which he combined evangelistic preaching and fund raising for the college, Baker decided that it would be best simply to preach the Word as he had done in his earlier ministry. He would let the people know of the needs of the college without any pressure and leave it to them to take up an offering for it at the end of the meetings if they saw fit. This methodology was greatly blessed, for in the last years of his life he raised over one hundred thousand dollars for the college (a huge amount in terms of buying power in the 1850s). Further, these last few years of his life witnessed a fresh outpouring of the Holy Spirit on his preaching with a consequent ingathering of souls which surpassed anything since the revival of 1831 and 1832.

Some of the greatest scenes of blessing during the last seven years of his life took place, not so much in Texas as in the older states of the South during preaching tours on behalf of Austin College. For instance, in the summer of 1852 he preached for nearly ten consecutive weeks in various locations in Low Country and in the Pee Dee area of South Carolina, often speaking three times a day. He was in Charleston, Kingstree, Sumter, Darlington, Marion, Bishopville, etc. He wrote to his wife from the Indiantown church (near Kingstree, S.C.) during this tour:

You may well suppose many tears of delicious joy were shed. We had a little jubilee, a pentecostal season in miniature . . . But I must look upon my heavenly Father as the great spring and source of all for he

> has blessed my preaching to the conversion of so many; only think! on an average something more perhaps than two converts for every sermon! and these chiefly men, young men of promise, and middle aged men, prominent men, as prominent and influential as any in the whole community.[61]

A year later, in 1853, Baker was again in the old states, this time in North Carolina. During this particular tour he witnessed the nearest thing to revival – affecting a whole community – that he had seen since 1832. There was a powerful spirit of conviction of sin and joy in a crucified Christ in and around the strongly Presbyterian 'Scotch-Irish' territory of Charlotte, North Carolina. Baker wrote to his wife on July 8, 1853:

> The meeting held at Charlotte was one of the most delightful I ever attended in all my life; forty-seven professed conversion, amongst whom were four lawyers, two physicians, six merchants, and a pretty large number of gay and fashionable young ladies – one an heiress![62]

Several days later, there was a tremendous gathering of people from the farms and villages outside Charlotte at Poplar Tent Church to hear Baker preach, even though it was a time of intense August heat and humidity. Baker writes:

> This warm weather, I can scarcely stand it! Last Sabbath I suppose that more than two thousand persons were present. I was obliged to preach in the open air; and being almost entirely overcome, I had actually to take my seat, and preach for a time sitting . . . Hearts opened – purses have been opened also [i.e. for Austin College], and in some cases (one in particular) the silvery stream flowing in, has been swollen to such an extent that I had to check it.[63]

Later, at Providence Church, the local minister believed one hundred and three to have been converted, most of those being grown men. From Steel Creek Church (which for many years – well into the twentieth century – was considered to be the largest rural Presbyterian church in America) Baker wrote:

> Immense congregations attend upon my preaching – every Sabbath perhaps three thousand. People come from a great distance, and I am told there has not been such a glorious revival in North Carolina for the last fifty years. To God be all the glory![64]

From the Piedmont interior part of the state, Baker went East to the Atlantic port city of Wilmington, where so many attended that the meetings could not be held inside the church. At this juncture Baker, who was spiritually thrilled, was also feeling the debilitating effects of a recent illness. He wrote:

. . . being unable to stand, I preached sitting, to some eight hundred persons in the grove. This meeting, as well as others, was crowned with a rich blessing. In the eleven protracted meetings which I have attended in North Carolina recently, something more than six hundred persons have been hopefully converted; of whom nearly three-fourths are males, from fourteen to seventy years of age. In some of these meetings, an unusually large number are heads of families; and I am happy to learn that the blessed work is going on, converts continuing to drop in after the special services were closed. It has been remarked, that there has not been such a revival of religion in North Carolina for fifty years. 'Not unto us, not unto us, but unto thy name, O Lord, be all the praise!'[65]

Although Daniel Baker had continued to be blessed with much physical stamina and a never-failingly clear, ringing voice into his old age, he began to experience dizzy spells from time to time during those final Carolina and Georgia tours. He seemed to sense that the end of his earthly life was rapidly drawing near. This sense that a loosing of moorings and a folding of the tent was near came poignantly upon him when he visited the site of his old home at Midway, Georgia, during his 1853 preaching tour in Low Country. He wrote movingly to his daughter:

I have visited once more the scenes of my nativity . . . [it] waked up in my bosom feelings both pleasant and mournful to my soul . . . Having not been there for some twenty-two years, I really felt that I was a stranger in a strange land, so many changes had taken place. I tried to find out the very spot where I first breathed the breath of life; but the house was gone, and the plough had passed over the place. All the shade-trees had disappeared, and not even a stump was left to mark my early romping-ground. The ditch, too, where with pin-hook and thread I was wont, in my childhood, to catch the perch and the beam, was filled up. Everything was changed, and so changed that I could scarcely recognize the place of my birth sixty-two years ago . . .
On Sabbath I cast my eyes over the congregation – everything was new – so many strange faces; and even the few known before had undergone surprising changes. Cheeks were furrowed which were smooth, and

locks had become almost as white as snow which had been black as a raven. It really seemed that I belonged to the men of another generation, and had come back from the spirit-land![66]

A year later he wrote to James McDowell, a young seminary student in Columbia, South Carolina:

As for myself, I may say, with one of old, 'It is toward evening, and the day is far spent.' But as my sun is setting, it is cheering to see other suns rising. How pleasant to think, that when the present generation of ministers shall have passed away, another generation will be raised up to take their place; and then, how happy, how glorious will the final meeting be![67]

Baker attended the General Assembly of the Old School Presbyterian Church in New York in 1856. The Assembly decided to publish his *Addresses to Little Children.* Also a new edition of his popular *Revival Sermons* was being prepared. After preaching in various Southeastern states, he crossed the Gulf back into Texas for the very last time. From a previous letter to a paper in Willington, South Carolina, we can gather an impression of what his thoughts may have been as he finally parted with his Old Southern homeland for his adopted home of Texas, where his sun would soon go down. We may well imagine that his thoughts were not of himself but of Christ and his kingdom:

I have been preaching Christ for nearly forty years, and in the contemplation of him I am more and more filled with wonder, admiration, and joy. Perhaps this may have given some new freshness, and power and unction and success to my preaching. 'O, that all but knew him!' In Christ there is a beauty that is unspeakable; there are wonders which human language cannot describe. If I may say so, in Christ there is an ocean of wonders. For, how wonderful, that he who was so rich, for our sakes became poor – so poor as to have no place to lay his head. How wonderful, that he who, in heaven, is the Savior of all, should for our sakes on earth, become a man of sorrows, and acquainted with grief! . . . This has been the principal theme of all my sermons, and hence what some are pleased to call the 'remarkable success' which has crowned my preaching. And to God be all the praise![68]

Daniel Baker was glad to be back home in Huntsville, Texas, after seeing hundreds pass into the kingdom and large sums raised which would ensure the continuance and prosperity of the college. Yet, concerning the last year of his life, after being at home and involved in the ordinary household routines, his son noted, 'sooner or later he became restless . . . the hand of his Master would lead him out again, a willing servant, to engage with fresh zeal in labors abroad.'[69] His last trip was from Huntsville to his son's home in Austin, in November 1857. The capital of Texas was at Austin, and Baker wished to contact the state legislators there concerning a grant for the college. Also he preached for his son, who was now the Presbyterian minister in Austin.

Although he was suffering from angina pectoris and was having to rest in his son's home, he managed to preach the last sermon of his life. It was the last Sunday night of November 1857. His son describes the scene:

> In rising to take his text at night, he remarked that he was about to preach a sermon which, if he knew when he was to die, he would choose as his last; and this because the sermon was full of Jesus Christ, to a degree unusual even in his preaching. It is Sermon III in the First Series of his *Revival Sermons*; preached in accordance with a request of an elder of the Austin church . . . He paused a moment after making the remark, as if considering what he had said, and then solemnly repeated the remark. And it was his last sermon![70]

A few days later, after a violent spell during the night, Baker obtained some relief from his physician. His son writes:

> When, at his request, his son prayed by his bedside for his recovery, he gently but decidedly rebuked him on rising. 'I asked you to pray for the presence of God with me, not for my recovery.'[71]

During the last few hours of his life on December 10th, he said to his son:

> William, my son, if I should die, I want this epitaph carved on my tomb – 'Here lies Daniel Baker, Preacher of the Gospel. A sinner saved by grace.' Remember, he added, A Sinner saved by Grace.[72]

His intellect was unclouded in the last moments of his earthly life and his assurance was strong and happy:

> . . . he lifted his eyes to heaven, and exclaimed, in the serene exercise of a perfect faith, 'Lord Jesus, into thy hands I commend my spirit!'

As the last word passed his lips, he closed his eyes on earth, to open them for ever on the face of that Savior, whom, not having seen, he so loved.[73]

Thus, he who had been privileged to experience revivals below passed to the place from which revivals come.

4

REVIVAL AND EVANGELISM

We must now consider briefly the significance of revival in Daniel Baker's itinerant ministry in the South and Southwest during the first half of the nineteenth century. As we have already noted earlier in this volume, there has been at least one revival in every century ever since the great revival known as the Protestant Reformation in the sixteenth century. The only century not to have seen major revival somewhere in the North Atlantic, Anglo-Saxon culture is our own – the twentieth. There was the Puritan revival and movement in the early seventeenth century, and then the 'First Great Awakening' (or 'Evangelical Revival') of the 1730s and 1740s, under Whitefield, Wesley, Edwards, the Tennents and many others.

We must place the times of reviving during Daniel Baker's earlier ministry in the latter part of the long, reviving period known as the 'Second Great Awakening.' This period stretched from approximately the late 1780s to the late 1830s and was marked by sporadic movements of the Spirit of God in geographically varied locations up and down the young American Republic. The less intense, but none the less evident, times of reviving experienced in Baker's Carolina tours in the later 1850s were possibly a foretaste of the short, but strong revival that was to start in Charleston, South Carolina and New York City about the same time in 1858. A similar time of blessing also occurred in Scotland, Wales and Northern Ireland, where it would be known as the 1859 Revival.

How would Daniel Baker have defined revival? His two volumes of published sermons are titled *Revival Sermons*, but in them he does not really give a formal definition of revival (although he defends revivals against their opposers in an appendix to his first volume).[74] Yet from his sermons and biography, I would conclude that Baker saw revival as a supernaturally powerful sense of God's reality and nearness together with a widespread attention to the convicting and gracious presence of the Holy Spirit.

This seems to accord with what was often said in the American colonies during the First Great Awakening, that revival was an unusual 'attention' to the things of God. And during the 1858–59 Revival much the same thing was meant when it was stated that there was a powerful consciousness of the presence of God throughout the community, thus putting every other human activity and value into its proper perspective, far below the pearl of great price.

It is not surprising that this man, who was so powerfully used to make others aware of the presence of God and thus give their whole-hearted attention to his truth, was himself keenly aware of the grace, kindness, beauty and joy of God's nearness. He regularly spent much time in the secret place with the Lord, and when he went to preach in a strange community he sought to go with a sense of God's presence upon him and an immense confidence in the infinite goodness and wonder-working power of his truth. His biographer states that, 'His effort was to present divine truth with transparent clearness, and let that truth work its own results.'[75] Baker's biographer could say of him what was rightly said of Charles H. Spurgeon, that he preached for the conversion of sinners, 'he expected them, and he saw them.'[76]

But the expectation that Baker (and Spurgeon) held that God would work as his truth was proclaimed to the people was of a very different order from the idea of the Arminian evangelist, Charles Finney, who held that proper human evangelistic actions and organization could guarantee salvation and revival. Baker of course knew of Finney, for Finney had belonged with the 'New School' Presbyterians before he had left the Presbyterian Church in 1836. Baker sided with the 'Old School' in that denomination's division in the following year. One of the tenets of the New School (or at least of such men as Albert Barnes and Finney) was that the Fall of Adam did not do such damage to the human personality as to render it incapable of responding to God any time it willed to do so. In contrast, when Baker got up to preach, he knew – and openly proclaimed – the utter inability of the fallen personality to do anything towards his own appropriation of salvation. In a sermon on 'The Duty of Coming to Christ' (John 6:44), Baker states:

And now, let us pause and contemplate the helpless and deplorable condition of the sinner, as one lying low in the ruins of the fall. He is under the reigning power of sin, and he cannot break the reigning power of sin . . . he is bound over to wrath, and he cannot help himself. Aye, he is in a state of nature and of sin, and his heart must be changed or he can never be saved; and of himself he can no more change his own heart than he can roll a mountain, or heave an ocean . . . such is the deep depravity of the sinner's heart . . . that no man can come to Christ, except he be divinely drawn. O, sinner, believe me, you are lost, ruined, and undone! You lie completely at the mercy of God![77]

Far from being depressed at man's inability to come to God, Baker was lifted up in hope and expectation as he preached to sinners because of what he knew about the God who had sent him to preach. Simply stated, he knew that there was a divine drawing, which was just as scripturally true as man's inability, for 'in the sacred volume they are linked together'[78]:

We may not be able to understand the operation fully, but I believe that a person may be under this system of divine drawing without being fully conscious of it, for oftentimes the influences of the Spirit are as gentle as the dew.[79]

Baker then went on to compare and contrast this divine drawing of the human personality with other kinds of drawing, and to give scriptural illustrations of it. Elsewhere, in terms taken directly from the Westminster Shorter Catechism, Baker deals with the drawing, regenerating work of the Spirit in the dawning consciousness of the believer, in which faith is thus being born. 'Yes, it is this faith, this precious faith, which unites us to Christ in our effectual calling; and it is this which guarantees our acquittal and our acceptance in the great day.'[80]

Baker knew that God would, as pleased him, draw helpless sinners to himself through the ordinances of preaching and prayer, because of his sovereign election of many to salvation. In a sermon on 'The Sovereignty of God,' Baker, among other texts, deals with the passage in Acts: 'As many as were ordained to eternal life believed.'

If the election of characters and not persons be intended, Luke made a slip of the pen, and should have said, As many as *believed* were *ordained* unto eternal life. But no! this is the way it is written, 'And as many as were ordained unto eternal life believed.' . . . Some object to the doctrine of election. Is it the *word*? It is in the Bible, in numerous places, and cannot be expunged. Is it the *principle*? . . . And what is this doctrine? I would define it thus: It is God's plan of securing the salvation of some, of a great multitude which no man can number! Now, why would we object to a plan for securing the salvation of a great multitude of the human family, which no man can number, when, without it, the salvation of all would be in jeopardy?[81]

Baker counted on the sovereign God to draw his elect to himself, and he also counted on the saints to love one another. Baker had a tender sensitivity to the duty of mutual love among Christians and a deep desire not to grieve the Spirit by lack of love. At a meeting in Circleville, Ohio, in the July of 1834, Baker wrote in his diary:

In the early part of the week, strove hard to bring about a reconciliation with certain professors, who, for some time, had been at variance with each other. All in vain. The Spirit's influence seemed gradually to be withdrawn; and at the close of the meeting . . . we had to lament that the sins of the professed people of God had prevented richer blessings.[82]

Another characteristic of Daniel Baker, that often seems to be present in men of revival, was the element of tender pleading with the lost, not unlike the attitude of the Apostle Paul in 2 Corinthians 5. How often Baker speaks of the shedding of tears over and with those to whom he was preaching. He felt the reality of eternal things and cared deeply for the people, and they knew it.

God chose to grant Baker the unction and to make those to whom he preached and over whom he prayed 'willing in the day of his power.' But at the same time, there is no reason to doubt that the continual prayerfulness of Baker, his endeavor to keep a conscience void of offense towards God and man, and his frequent calling of special concerts of prayer among the saints for the outpouring of the Spirit had a part to play in the scenes of glory that followed. And can we doubt that it was the Spirit himself who implanted those deep, lifelong urges to prayerfulness and holiness?

The lasting fruits of these times of awakening were evident for all to see. One observer at Beaufort, South Carolina, noted that the effects of the 1832 revival were still evident over twenty years later. Many years later, a leading Episcopal churchman stated the lasting effects on his denomination of Baker's revival:

> That party, the evangelical party, has now the ascendancy in the diocese of South Carolina. The same party has the ascendancy in the diocese of Georgia, its chosen leader, Bishop Elliott, acknowledging Mr. Baker as his spiritual father.[83]

If we consider the scenes of revival, the human actions and methodology that were employed during the First and Second Great Awakenings and the 1858–59 Revival, and compare it with the modern attempts to produce revival since the time of Dwight L. Moody in the 1870s, there seems to be a great divide. The earlier revivals looked to God to set the seal on his own Word as it was prayed over and proclaimed. In contrast, much of evangelicalism after Moody felt it proper to aid in this process by setting up 'anxious seats', inviting people to inquiry rooms, or asking them to raise their hands or walk to the front.[84] Although Daniel Baker clearly stood with the older Reformed tradition theologically, some aspects of his own methodology indicate that he was, without knowing it, a transitional figure in this direction.

Baker began his early ministry with an exclusion of what he called 'all machinery' – in other words, any tactic besides the preaching alone designed to generate a response from the hearers. During a time of quickening in the late 1820s, while he was still a minister in Washington, Dr Stephen Collins, one of Baker's elders and a medical doctor, made this observation:

> Ministers from abroad labored there with great zeal; perhaps not always with entire discretion. In the church of Dr. Baker the means employed were frequent meetings for prayer, private visitation, and

personal conversation. We excluded all 'machinery,' in the popular acceptation of the word. The result was a deep and quiet religious impression among the people, and a large accession to the membership of the church . . . If on application for admission, the case was doubtful, or too recent, the Session held it for further consideration.[85]

By the time of his pastorate in Savannah, Baker did take up the practice of inviting the unconverted to a lecture-room in order to preach to them 'the necessity of a sound conversion.'[86] In an Appendix to Volume I of his *Revival Sermons* (written in answer to a letter in 1835), Baker discusses his methodology:

. . . my rule has been to confine myself to no set of measures whatever; for my opinion has been and still is, that a measure which might be useful in one place, may be positively injurious in another. I have therefore varied them, according to times and places and circumstances. My general plan in conducting a protracted meeting has been this: After the first sermon, I come down from the pulpit, and address professors of religion, who are respectfully requested to occupy the seats immediately in front. This *measure*, if you choose to term it such, has usually had a remarkably happy effect. After the second or third sermon, (I) come down from the pulpit again, and address the youth grouped in the same way . . .
When certain individuals are known to be under serious impressions, an invitation is sometimes given, on peculiarly solemn occasions, for those who are serious, and who desire an interest in the prayers of God's people, to come forward, or kneel at their seats.

Then, Baker goes on to admit that at this point he had changed his views concerning methodology from earlier days:

This measure I once did not approve; but experience has taught me that it has a tendency to break down the pride of the heart, give decision of character, encourage ministers, and rouse the people of God to more earnest and effectual prayer.[87]

At this point, Baker appears to give no theological justification for this change, merely a pragmatic one. Perhaps Baker's lack of a higher theological education in Princeton, Columbia or Union may have left him less inclined to think through such measures theologically in the light of his undoubtedly Calvinist convictions about man's inability and the Spirit's drawing. Or perhaps he saw no inconsistency between this measure and his view of God's sovereignty in salvation. This writer cannot say.

But what we can be sure of is that Baker's change of methodology had some influence on later trends in American (and then British) evangelism, which were far more consonant with Arminian than Calvinist premises.

Baker's influence was especially felt by Dwight L. Moody, who – according to William H. Benchoff – in his early Christian life literally memorized many of the sermons of Daniel Baker.[88] In later years, Moody had Baker's sermons reprinted in Britain, while he was there on his long evangelistic mission. Moody would certainly have read Baker's Appendix on his changed view of methodology.

Certainly it would be unfair and anachronistic to read back the modern evangelistic assumptions involved in 'the invitation system' into the ministry of Daniel Baker. His sermons and his biography indicate that he would have been appalled at much that passes for true evangelism in the twentieth century. And what is more, it seems patently clear that very few evangelists today would be prepared to preach the same old gospel which he preached. A contemporary minister of Harmony Presbytery (in Low Country and the Pee Dee area of South Carolina) stated that Baker's adherence to the old gospel, far from hindering the progress of revival, furthered it:

> It is especially gratifying to state that the distinctive points of our Old-School theology were clearly, fully, and faithfully preached. It has been imagined that these are calculated to check the progress of a revival, and have therefore been avoided on such occasions . . . I think the religious movement among us is due mainly to the plain . . . presentation of these great doctrines in their own solemn Scripture attire. The sovereign purpose of God in election, the vicarious atonement of Christ, the total inability of the sinner, the instantaneous work of regeneration, the perseverance of the saints; these in all their glorious beauty and sweetness, to the believer, in all their startling terror to the sinner, were set forth, without reserve as the counsel of God.[89]

This same minister from Harmony Presbytery went on to state that:

> No 'new measures' were resorted to in order to arouse the feelings. These were rendered unnecessary by the Spirit of God.[90]

And yet this report was made late in Baker's career, when he definitely did practice the call for people to kneel or come to an inquiry room. So whether these 'measures' were not taken while he was in Harmony Presbytery, or whether his fellow conservative minister considered these a part of normal church procedure, or whether perhaps the term 'new measures' referred to the emotional atmosphere of Methodist camp meetings (such as the nearby Indianfield Methodist Campground in St George, South Carolina) it is now impossible to say. The crucial issue in 'new measures' evangelism seems to be the employment of various techniques to induce 'decisions'. In my opinion, Baker did not knowingly intend to do this. But what we cannot doubt is that Baker, in spite of his transitional methodological procedures, fearlessly, faithfully and fruitfully proclaimed the old gospel of Calvin, Knox, Witherspoon, Davies and Alexander. And the God of truth and grace set his seal on Baker's preaching as he had done to that of Calvin, Knox and the others.

5

THE JOYFUL PREACHER

It remains for us now to consider specific features of the preaching of Daniel Baker, which the God of the covenant so signally honored.

The first characteristic of his preaching that has struck me as I have read through all of his extant sermons is the same characteristic that is so evident as one studies his personal life: joy. Once when preaching against the idea that 'religion is a gloomy thing,' Baker spoke of the joy of the young convert:

> Religion a gloomy thing! – has no charms for you! Look at the young convert, how his eyes sparkle! how every feature beams with joy! Hark, how his tongue breaks out in songs of praise . . .
> But suppose there be no rapture, the young convert has a sweet complacency in Christ – a heavenly calm, and the peace of God . . . It gives us a scriptural assurance that our sins are forgiven for Jesus' sake. Is there anything in this to sadden the heart?[91]

In another sermon, he deals with that inner joy of the true believer, which does not depend on outward circumstances. What he says here must surely be reminiscent of his own many years of 'joy unspeakable and full of glory':

> See for example, Paul and Silas at Philippi. They are shamefully treated . . . they are beaten . . . Surely, they are the most wretched persons in Philippi! It is a mistake. They are the happiest – the very happiest! They are too happy to sleep! for, we are told, that 'at midnight, Paul and Silas prayed and sang praises unto God.' . . . their inward consolations are so great! . . . They are happy! They are joyful! They forget that the gloom of the inner prison is around them.

Celestial radiance is beaming in direct upon their souls! They forget that their feet are made fast in the stocks; they seem to be walking in a large place!
. . . The full tide of heavenly consolation is flowing into every chamber of their souls! . . . How can this be accounted for? . . . they have full evidence that they are the children of God; that God loves them; and that soon their 'weary feet shall reach the peaceful inn of lasting rest.'. . . Only a little while, and they will be looking their Redeemer in the face with joy! . . . How beautifully . . . does this illustrate our text – 'Let every man prove his own work, and then shall he have rejoicing in himself alone, and not in another.'[92]

Baker's preaching was full of joy because he had a deep, clear and convinced sense of the gospel. A certain type of preaching easily inculcates superficial happiness because of light views of sin, wrath, death and hell. Contrary to this, Baker's preaching saw sin in all its sinfulness and God in all his holiness, and thus the inexorable and utterly righteous requirement for the propitiation of infinite wrath against infinite guilt. Baker shows how the agonies of Christ's death make impossible any light views of sin and infinite guilt:

But O! the tears, the groans, the streaming blood and dying agonies of the great Redeemer, Jehovah's Equal, God's Eternal Son, will sound the notes of warning louder still. If God spared not his own Son, when he was found in the law's place, and stead of the sinner, will he spare any sinner who has to answer for himself? Justice of heaven! How inflexible dost thou appear when thy glittering sword is bathed in Immanuel's blood! in the blood of an incarnate God![93]

Baker's preaching shows that he had read, studied and thought long, deep and hard about the foundational truths entering into the gospel way of salvation. His sermon on 'Christ the Mediator' (Philippians 2:6–11) is a model of both theologically profound and devotionally applicatory gospel preaching. In it he deals effectively, clearly and movingly with something parish ministers (not to mention media evangelists) generally appear to steer clear of: '. . . that Jesus Christ, as Mediator, possesses two natures – the divine and the human – in mysterious, yet all-harmonious union.' He states why he would preach on such a complex subject to the ordinary people of God:

This is a doctrine of prime importance. It lies at the very foundation of the whole Christian system; and with it, the most precious hopes of the believer must live or die.[94]

In Sermon VII of his Second Volume, he deals effectively with this same theme of '. . . the two-fold nature – the divine and the human – in mysterious, yet all-harmonious union,' in relation to the sufferings of Christ.[95]

To state that Baker had deep and clear views of the gospel in his preaching is another way of saying that his preaching was full of the biblical Christ. Late in his life, Baker wrote a letter to his son, answering the question as to why God has blessed his preaching. He replied:

If you ask why my preaching is so much blessed, I say again, 'Even so, Father, for so it seemed good in thy sight.' But if it will throw any light upon the subject, I will tell you that my plan is incessantly to preach Christ and him crucified; and this I do in an earnest, colloquial manner, and not infrequently, streaming tears attest the sincere and tender feelings of my own heart, aiming at the conversion of sinners. Being earnest and colloquial, I have the more fixed attention . . . take a burning glass, and let the object, at the proper focal distance, remain in a fixed position, and it soon begins to smoke. So the mind, kept in contact with divine truth pouring upon it, soon begins to warm and kindle up . . . Now, preaching Christ so much, I keep upon my own mind a more distinct . . . impression of his wonderful love and compassion for our ruined race . . . God is a Sovereign, but he generally works by appropriate means.[96]

In another context, Baker said this about sermon content:

Indeed, in my opinion, the sermon which does not present the blessed Savior, is no better than a cloud without water, a shadow without the substance, a casket without the jewel, a body without the soul. Yes, it is Christ, and Christ crucified, which gives beauty and efficiency to every thing . . . According to the Scriptures, in the economy of redemption, Christ is all in all.[97]

While speaking earlier of his preaching in the context of revivals, we noted that his proclamation was unmistakably 'Old School' as it upheld the sovereignty of God's grace in the gospel. In other words, his preaching was clearly Calvinistic, for the Christ whom he presented was not a weak, pathetic figure, standing outside the door, begging to come in, cap in hand. Rather, for all his emphasis on the tender-hearted blood-and-tear sufferings of our brother in the flesh, the Man of Sorrows, he lifted up the risen, crowned, reigning and conquering Lion of the tribe of Judah who is ever going forth in the ordinances of his Word and in the providences of history 'conquering and to conquer.'

Baker understood that for a full and free offer of the biblical gospel and of the blessings available through vital union with 'the Man in the glory', a solid and irreducible theological structure is required within which the offer can be made. To cut out part of the biblically given structure to avoid offending the pride of man is a counter-productive measure that can eventually lead to the loss of the gospel itself, and thus of all hope for the humanity whom one originally set out to help.

Referring to two of his sermons, 'The Duty of Coming to Christ' and 'The Sovereignty of God', his biographer states:

> Dr. Baker presented these doctrines so clearly . . . as to make it evident that they are indeed the gospel itself, in all its freeness and fullness, in all its sweetness and power. His whole aim was to do as Scripture does – exalt God and humble man – place the almighty Sovereign and the offending subject in their actual relations to each other; and this in order to show how infinite the love of God in stooping to save, and how absolutely essential the need, and certain the salvation of such a Savior.[98]

The minister of the Presbyterian church in Darlington, South Carolina, wrote on October 14th, 1852:

> Dr. Baker's preaching is eminently Calvinistic. The doctrines of our Church – the divine sovereignty, election, total depravity, vicarious atonement, and efficacious grace, were prominently exhibited . . . Great stillness and solemnity characterized the large assemblies . . . a sea of uplifted faces, with many streaming eyes, directed towards the speaker, as the words of eternal life fell from his lips.[99]

Baker himself in his sermon on the sovereignty of God stated:

> . . . the longer I live, and the more carefully I examine the subject, the more thoroughly convinced am I, that the system, usually termed Calvinistic, is firmly based upon the Bible . . . the system needs only to be correctly understood by all the true people of God, to be received and loved.[100]

Once when he was preaching in Lagrange, Texas, which – along with neighboring Bastrop, Texas – had apparently been influenced by the Cumberland Presbyterians (who as a denomination rejected the more 'Calvinist' portions of the Westminster Confession), Baker perceived '. . . that the distinctive doctrines of our communion were sadly misapprehended in this region.' Thus he preached 'a long doctrinal sermon' which he believed 'happily removed many prejudices and did much good.'[101] In doing so, he was not being narrowly denominational, for as we have seen he gladly preached in and worked with churches of other denominations (as in the revival in Beaufort, South Carolina), but his intention was to safeguard the very foundation and structure of the gospel of grace which he so gladly offered to his generation.

In addition to joy and solid theological structure, another characteristic which stands out in Daniel Baker's preaching is its friendly quality. People who heard him preach received the distinct impression that here was a man who was very friendly towards them, who was literally laying himself out to do them good for time and eternity. This friendly quality is not always evident, even in preaching that is technically biblical and Calvinistic. But where it is evident and where it is combined with a clear grasp of the truth of the gospel, it will receive a hearing and a good hearing – often from those most prejudiced against the truth.

A man who later became a leading politician in Washington once said this about Baker's preaching:

> 'Excellent, excellent,' said he. 'Then of course, you will hear him again?' 'No,' he replied. 'I am bound to occupy a seat in the Senate of the United States, and if I go to hear him again he'll spoil it all.' This gentleman was, however, persuaded to hear him again, and on conversing with him next day, he said, 'I can stand your fire and brimstone preachers very well, but this man makes me cry, and I must keep out of his way, or he will make a saint out of me.'[102]

The comments of a minister in Tallahassee, Florida, express the almost universal impression of Baker's audiences across the land:

> His appeals were so kind, so earnest, so evidently sincere, that, whatever other effects they produced, his impenitent hearers could

not resist the impression that the speaker was their friend. And this was one secret, so far as human agency was concerned, of his great power over his audience.[103]

The many congregations that heard Baker preach were impressed not only with his friendly attitude towards them, but also with the fact that he was talking good, common sense, which therefore deserved their careful attention as sensible persons. One of Baker's frequent maxims was, 'A grain of common sense is an excellent thing,'[104] and he preached to people in a way that convinced them his message was eminently sensible and that to reject it was eminently foolish and self-destructive. That is perhaps the reason why he had so much success in winning Deists and atheists to Christ. In one sermon he speaks of how opposition to God is 'an unreasonable war,'[105] in another, he movingly demonstrates how frightfully self-destructive it is to delay seeking reconciliation with God.[106] It was often noticed that a large percentage of Baker's converts were grown men. His way of talking sense obviously appealed to them. Is it possible that the general lack of men in so many of our churches today could have something to do with the absence of this quality in preaching?

At this point we will do well to look at some of the technical, mechanical aspects of Baker's sermons, in order to see just how he took the truth of God and made it sensible to the people of his day. From contemporary accounts, it was felt that, although lacking in high oratorical ability, his preaching was structured and presented in a way that enabled his hearers easily to follow the logic of his thought. One who often heard him preach in his later years said:

> I have heard more finished orators . . . but I have seldom heard an orator who made his hearers understand him better, or who gave them less room, or less occasion, in fact, to dodge the conclusions to which he came. He is composed, and thoroughly in earnest. He seems himself to follow the track along which he leads you . . .[107]

Baker's sermons were easy to follow because they were clearly structured. His sermon on 'The Sufferings of Christ, and Their Design' is simply and effectively outlined as follows:

I Who is this sufferer?

II What did he suffer?
III For whom, or what did he suffer?[108]

His sermon on 'The Sovereignty of God' is outlined as follows:

I In creation.
II In preservation.
III In the perfections of God.

Then (perhaps a subheading of III or perhaps a new heading):

'Distinguishing features of the government of God'
1 It is supreme and universal.
2 It is particular.
3 It extends not only to all things, but to all events; not only to all creatures, but to all their actions.
4 It is absolute.
5 It is wise and good.[109]

A good outline is not sufficient, of course, to accomplish the goals of evangelical preaching. As a preacher moves through his outline, he must strive to focus the thoughts of his congregation, with an ever-increasing momentum as he progresses towards the end of the sermon. But not only will he seek to engage their minds, but also both to touch their emotions and to move their will in a Godward direction. Though it is all but impossible to put on paper exactly how to do that, a close reading of Baker's sermons will show that he did it and how he did it. His sermon on 'The Fulfillment of Scripture Prophecy' (Volume II) is a good model in this regard and, indeed, it is characteristic of nearly all of his sermons. As a professor of theology, and one who frequently hears the sermons of others (nearly always with much personal benefit), it seems to me that this is an important quality often lacking in young preachers: the ability to focus thought down to a point, like driving a widely scattered herd of cattle together and pressing them through a narrow gate so that they proceed at last in orderly fashion into their destination for the night.

Baker helps herd his congregation into the narrow gate, not only by structure and focused movement, but also by the use of clear, plain and attractive English. For instance:

I have seen sinners coming to Christ. I have seen them in the day of their conversion. O what a blessed moment! what a glorious change! The soul has new feelings; the heart has new joy! Everything within is pleasant; every thing around is lovely. The sun shines more brightly, and the birds sing more sweetly. The flowers are more beautiful, and even the grass looks more green . . . Sometimes the young convert feels as if he had entered into a new world . . .[110]

Even when dealing with deeply complex subjects like the hypostatic union of the two natures in the one person of Christ,[111] the divine drawing of the elect, but spiritually dead sinner,[112] Baker is a master of concise, understandable English. Preachers who are determined to proclaim the whole counsel of God to their people in a comprehensible way would do well to study some of these sermons of Daniel Baker.

Baker is able to take his audience along with him in the direction dictated by God's truth partly because of his vivid style and his employment of illustrations and parables from everyday life. He certainly lacks John L. Girardeau's remarkable ability to paint almost Rembrandt-like word pictures, but how vivid are his descriptions of the brevity of life;[113] his visit to a graveyard;[114] a little dying boy's request to his father to cease swearing;[115] and of sudden death.[116] In my opinion he does not over-illustrate, but how apt are his homely and often touching and engaging parables of truth in Georgia, Carolina and Texas clothes!

His illustrations are not merely local or national, but like all true preaching which pierces the human heart, universal:

When death comes, we cease to be interested in all the exciting scenes of earth. A new star may be discovered . . . but a Sir Isaac Newton or a Kepler, wrapped in the winding-sheet and laid in the grave, takes no interest in this newly discovered star . . . Aye, and even the tender mother, who, as she was sinking in the arms of death, said, Bring me my sweet babe, and kissed it . . . that mother buried may the very next day have her grave opened, and that child, wrapped in its little winding-sheet, may be brought and laid upon its mother's bosom in the grave, and even the tender mother greets not her once darling child. How deep are the slumbers of the dead![117]

Baker also puts to good use the effective preaching device of contrast. He ably makes important points by contrasting faith and unbelief;[118] works' righteousness versus faith;[119] and the different experiences in death of infidels and believers.[120]

Like John Calvin, one of the strong points of his colloquial preaching was that he addressed various groups of his hearers very specifically, directly, and – undoubtedly at times – uncomfortably, in order 'to smoke them out' of their hiding places. The way he deals with excuses which people make to keep from facing the claims of God on their lives must have caused many in his congregation to feel he had somehow overheard their thoughts![121] He speaks in a direct, demanding and friendly way to definite classes of hearers: to sinners;[122] to respectable persons;[123] to youth;[124] and to parents.[125] On a number of occasions, many who heard him stated, 'It was not in human hearts to resist influence that awoke its sympathies and spoke its purest and most elevated policy.'[126] Dr John Miller Wells, speaking of Baker's awareness of and careful attention to the different sorts of people who were before him, said: 'To all of these classes he brought earnest exhortations suited to them.'[127]

Joy, sound theological structure, focused movement, clear vivid language and touching illustrations were all strong points of Baker's preaching which enabled him to make the truth of God take on flesh and blood in the lives of his generation. But, like the efforts of all fallen men, Baker's preaching was not without its weak points. Some of his sermons deal with the details and larger ramifications of a biblical text within its own precise context. He takes a text, and what he says about it is true, but often his main points, true as they are, are taken from other portions of Scripture, so that he effectively misses the major thrust of the text and larger passage in hand. That is certainly the case in his sermons on faith[128] and justification,[129] though he does a better textual job on 'The Divine Drawing to Christ' (from John 6:44).[130]

Serious as this weakness was, he nevertheless followed the advice of the famous professor whom he knew when he was a student at Princeton, Archibald Alexander. In his *Thoughts on Religious Experience*, Professor Alexander advised preachers 'to make your sermons full of Scripture, for the Scriptures have converted more atheists than all the books of evidences that exist.' We cannot doubt that better exegetical procedure would have made his sermons stronger, but we can rejoice at the converting power they did have because of their faithfulness to and fulness of Scripture.

Other than the quiet and obvious joy that meets you at nearly every turn of his preaching, there is a further property that impresses itself constantly upon one who goes through his sermons: it is the atmosphere of eternity that catches us unawares and upsets all our lesser values. In our hedonistic age when it is widely accepted that true joy and meaning in life are to be found in the pleasures which material things and merely physical relationships can provide, it catches us off guard to be reminded of the main business of life:

> God Almighty never sent us into this world merely that we might plant, and build, and buy and sell, and get gain, and then go and sleep an everlasting sleep in the grave. How much less did he send us into this world that we might run the round of worldly pleasure and fashion, and sin and folly, and then drop into the pit which has no bottom! O no! Man has an immortal soul, and a higher destiny awaits him. He is to prepare for another and a better world. According to the Scriptures there is a heaven. O heaven, sweet heaven! The purchase of a Savior's blood, the Christian's rest, the pilgrim's home, the dwelling place of love, of glory and of God![131]

Baker has a way of taking the solemn scenes of eternity and bringing them 'in living color' into our present occupations and material interests, which tend to 'drug' and deaden our sensitivity to the true interests of the soul – until awakened by a voice from beyond:

> And he [i.e. the 'fool' who rejected salvation] will remember – what? Why, that when on earth he preferred the interests of the body to the interests of the soul. By that time he will have seen the body turned over to corruption and the worm, and now he sees the soul in all its capacity for happiness and misery; he sees the souls of the righteous robed and crowned, rising and shining, and coruscating in glory unspeakable; and sees the souls of the wicked shrouded in darkness and despair . . . what must be his feelings to remember that when on earth he preferred the interests of that poor dying body that had to lie down in the grave, to that soul so mighty to sustain an exceeding great and eternal weight of glory, or an exceeding great and eternal weight of sorrow?[132]

Surely, the two leading characteristics of this great evangelist – glad tidings and swift and beautiful feet – worked so powerfully in him because of the nearness and reality of his own soul to eternity and to him who sits upon the throne. In the light of this obvious connection between conviction of eternity and obedient Christian service, a few simple and sincere questions could beneficially be asked of us, who are today's Christian laymen and preachers.

What do we believe to be the main business of life? Do we believe that people are truly and eternally lost if they die without Jesus Christ? Are we happy enough about the gospel to spend our resources in order to take the message with swift feet to where today's lost multitudes are congregated? Have we enough joy in God and his gospel for our life to be a quiet recommendation for the tidings we profess? If so, later generations may rise up and say of us what we can truly say of the life and travels and preaching of Daniel Baker: 'How beautiful upon the mountains are the feet of him that bringeth good tidings, that publisheth peace; that bringeth good tidings of good, that publisheth salvation; that saith unto Zion, Thy God reigneth!'

PART TWO

JAMES HENLEY THORNWELL: LOGIC ON FIRE

6

THE HONING OF AN INTELLECT FOR SERVICE TO CHURCH, STATE AND EDUCATION

The prophet Jeremiah speaks in one passage of the Word of the Lord as being like a 'fire and a hammer' (23:29) and in another says that the Word he was commanded to proclaim was like a 'fire in his own bones' (20:9). This quality of holy, consuming fire is the image most frequently alluded to by those who knew best the mighty preaching of James H. Thornwell. For instance, it was one of his closest friends and later his biographer, B. M. Palmer (also a true prince of the pulpit), who portrayed Thornwell's preaching as follows:

> The feature most remarkable in this prince of pulpit orators was the rare union of vigorous logic with strong emotion. He reasoned always, but never coldly. He did not present truth in what Bacon calls 'the dry light of the understanding'; clear, indeed, but without the heat which warms and fructifies. Dr. Thornwell wove his argument in fire. His mind warmed with the friction of his own thoughts, and glowed with the rapidity of his own motion; and the speaker was borne along in what seemed to others a chariot of flame . . .
>
> Kindling with a secret inspiration his manner lost its slight constraint; all angularity of gesture and awkwardness of posture suddenly disappeared; the spasmodic shaking of the head entirely ceased; his slender form dilated; his deep gray eye lost its drooping expression; the soul came and looked forth, lighting it up with a strange brilliancy; his frail body rocked and trembled as under a divine afflatus, as though the impatient spirit would rend its tabernacle and fly forth to God and heaven upon the wings of his impassioned words; until his fiery eloquence rising with the greatness of his conceptions, burst upon the hearers in some grand climax, overwhelming in its majesty and resistless in its effect . . .

[He was] . . . stirred by vigor of argument fused by a seraphic glow and pouring itself forth in strains which linger in the memory like the chant of angels.[1]

What was the background of such a man in whom the fire burned so brightly that his preaching, by all reports, seems to have been the releasing of a pent-up stream of sacred rhetoric on fire?

James Henley Thornwell was born on December 9, 1812, in the upcountry area of Marlboro County, South Carolina, the son of a plantation overseer who died when James was young. James' mother was a Calvinist Baptist, part of the Welsh Neck Baptist colony in the Society Hill area and in later years he would testify that his poor, though devout, Christian mother taught him the basic doctrines of grace.[2]

Young Thornwell showed remarkable intellectual abilities, which attracted the appreciative and sympathetic attention of some wealthy and generous planters and lawyers near Cheraw who decided to finance his education. It was assumed he would prepare for a career in law, but even before his conversion, his all-consuming earnestness and self-sacrificial spirit became evident when, at the age of sixteen, he felt called to be a minister. In a 'chance' conversation at the time, he happened to overhear some of his patrons saying that he should be a lawyer. This threw him into a terrible dilemma, because, in the words of Dr Thomas Law:

. . . so overwhelming was his conviction at that time, though not then himself a professing Christian, that he must prepare for the gospel ministry, even though it involved, as he apprehended, the sundering of the affectionate and delightful relations with his noble patrons and his loss of their needed help in his education, he felt constrained to inform Mr Robbins; and, unable to talk to him face to face about the matter, he wrote a manly, courageous letter, unfolding his views and convictions; and, putting it under Mr Robbins' plate at the supper table, hid himself until the dreaded revelation should occur.

Mr Robbins read it, and hunting his missing protégé, found him hiding on the piazza and weeping as if his heart would break. But, noble and wise man that he was, he took James by the hand and led him back to his accustomed place, and comforted his anxious heart with the assurance that no obstacle would be put in the way of his complying with his convictions of duty, and that the kindly relations between him and his patrons should not be disturbed on that account.[3]

Young Thornwell's future success in studies and in professional life would be based on intellect, hard work and providential blessing, for as one of his college classmates remembered him, he was not a man of impressive physical looks:

In personal appearance he was, perhaps, the most unpromising specimen of humanity that ever entered such an institution. Very short in stature, shorter by a head than he became later in life, very lean in flesh, with a skin the color of old parchment, his hands and face as thickly studded with black freckles as the Milky Way with stars, and an eye rendered dull in repose by a drooping lid, he looked, to use an Irishism, as if he was twenty years old when he was born.[4]

But as James O. Farmer has written: 'Yet references to Thornwell during his college years, as thereafter, rarely concentrate on his physical appearance; his intellect and personality made the major impression . . . Physically he was . . . an unlikely candidate for greatness. Small and frail, he weighed barely one hundred pounds. Friends expressed concern over his 'fleshless frame' and urged him to 'nurse [his body] a little.' His shoulders drooped, as did his eyelids. But intellectually he felt himself the match for any man, and his ego seems not to have suffered on account of his physical appearance.'[5]

Eventually Thornwell went to the leading educational institution of South Carolina, which was, at that time, South Carolina College (now University) in Columbia. Some historians, indeed, have compared its library and faculty with those of Yale during this period of its existence. At the age of nineteen, Thornwell demonstrated that his patrons' faith in him was well founded, and he graduated at the very top of his class. His first job was as a school teacher in Sumter, and it was here that he was converted and joined the Presbyterian Church. He became a Presbyterian instead of Baptist or perhaps Episcopalian, because one afternoon while browsing in a Columbia bookstore, he happened upon a copy of the Westminster Confession of Faith, which he bought. So fascinated was he by this document that he stayed up all night studying it, and in the months thereafter, had his whole thinking transformed by it.[6]

Soon afterwards, Thornwell finally decided to begin his preparation for the ministry. Instead of going to the recently formed Columbia Seminary in his own capital city, he felt he could get a better education in New England. Because he particularly wished to get a thorough grounding in Hebrew, Aramaic and German, he attended Andover for a while, and then Harvard. However, the discerning young theological student was so disturbed by the New School Theology as well as the prevalent Unitarianism of those institutions, that he eventually decided to return to Columbia Seminary. After graduation, he was licensed by Harmony Presbytery in 1834, and soon afterwards began his first pastorate at Lancaster, where he also preached in the nearby country churches of Waxhaw and Six-Mile Creek.

Perhaps like the young Martin Luther, who was stricken with awe before attempting to say his first mass, or more certainly like the Apostle Paul who trembled before preaching the evangel (1 Corinthians 2:3), we are told that the young preacher Thornwell nearly drew back from his first preaching engagement at Lancaster:

> But the crisis came as he entered the pulpit and began the service. Light from above then beamed in upon him, peace and joy filled his soul, and the Spirit of God unloosed his fettered lips. The question was settled, the victory was won, the divine anointing was bestowed; and the charmed hearers bore testimony to his power. And from that momentous hour he was a minister called and owned of the Lord.[7]

As Thornwell writes in a letter to wrote to his old patron, General Gillespie, at this time:

> I felt that a new era had commenced in my life in that I was no longer a citizen of the world, but an ambassador of God, standing in the stead of Jesus Christ and beseeching men to turn from the unsatisfying vanities of a fleeting life and to fix their hopes on the enduring sources of beatitude which surrounds the throne of God.[8]

Although he had been disappointed in an earlier romance, owing in part to his poor financial prospects, providence now smiled upon him as he became engaged, during his first pastorate, to a daughter of one of the leading families of Lancaster District. In 1835, he married Nancy White Witherspoon, a great-niece of the famous John Witherspoon of Scotland and Princeton, and daughter of Colonel James H. Witherspoon of Lancaster, South Carolina. 'Colonel Witherspoon was one of the leading men in the District, and not without distinction in the State; having served as Lieutenant-Governor, and was a candidate for Congress, with every prospect of being elected, when he was stricken by paralysis, which terminated in death.'[9] His father-in-law did not let Thornwell's small salary of six hundred dollars a year prevent his approval of the marriage, for – in the words of Palmer – 'he could not refuse domestic alliance to a young man whom he openly proclaimed intellectually the equal of . . . [Senator] John C. Calhoun.'[10]

According to the *Genealogy of the Witherspoon Family*, Nancy Witherspoon was 27 at the time of her marriage to James Thornwell, who was then 23. She is described by the *Genealogy* as 'tall, and of a large frame, with unusual force of character . . . firm as a rock and yet kind and loving.'[11] Thornwell's biographer, who knew them both intimately, described how well-suited Nancy was to her scholarly husband's temperament:

> By this union, a true helpmeet was provided for one whose gifts and whose calling required that he should not be entangled in the things of this life. Mrs. Thornwell's sound judgment and practical wisdom were a valuable check upon the ardent temperament and too confiding generosity of her husband. Her prudence and skilful management released him from domestic cares, to meet the exactions of his public station; while her womanly grace and cheerful disposition threw a serene charm about his home, in which his spirits found always a perfect repose.[12]

Thornwell more than once said: 'I have long known that I have the best wife in the world . . .'[13] and his many affectionate letters to her over the years indicate that their marriage was one of joy and love. It was not one without its sorrows, however, for four of their nine children died before their father, including their firstborn son, who died at the age of three months. The Witherspoon family gave the Thornwells a plantation near Lancaster, which James Thornwell enjoyed visiting for the rest of his life, especially during the long summer holidays from the South Carolina College, to which he was soon to go.

After only two years at Lancaster, at the age of twenty-five, Thornwell was elected Professor of Logic and Belles Lettres in South Carolina College. After holding this post for only two years, he was then called to be pastor of the influential First Presbyterian Church of Columbia and felt he should make the move. Through this pastorate his preaching abilities became widely known but in another year, he was called back to the college to be its chaplain, as well as Professor of Sacred Literature and Evidences of Christianity. It was then that he realized that he did enjoy the academic life and he accepted the position since it would offer him the opportunity happily and fruitfully to combine his calling to preach with his strong academic capabilities. Undoubtedly, one major reason why he would exchange the pulpit for the university was his understanding of the strategic importance of South Carolina College in educating the leadership of his state. At this time, the college was in transition from the administration of the Deist (or perhaps even atheist) Thomas Cooper to a conservative régime. Thus Thornwell was to play a large part in the purging and reconstruction of this pivotal South Carolina cultural and educational institution.

His only other pastorate was for a brief time in Charleston in 1851, but no sooner had he settled in than he was called back again as chaplain, but also this time as President of South Carolina College. The prestige of this position in antebellum society was very great: according to Hollis' *University of South Carolina*, it was 'one of the most prominent and sought-after positions in the State. In prestige it ranked just behind the United States Senatorships and the governorship.'[14]

It is interesting to think of the contrast between the impoverished rural orphan boy of Cheraw and the distinguished President of South Carolina College some thirty years later. There is no doubt that as a youth Thornwell was extremely ambitious, and in modern terms could be described as an over-achiever. Robert L. Dabney relates that General Thomas J. 'Stonewall' Jackson was the same before his conversion. But the grace of God transmuted the aching pride of man-centered ambition in both men into a profoundly humble, yet constantly energetic God-centered moral energy in the service of Christ's kingdom.

For all his energy and achievements, Thornwell never became a harsh professional with no time for ordinary people. On the contrary, the students found him to be very approachable and thoroughly human:

> Dr. Thornwell . . . commanded the love of young men by the fullness of his sympathy in their struggles with temptations and defeats, in their aspirations, their hopes, their joys. His disposition was thoroughly genial and affectionate. He never wrapped himself in the artificial dignity which repels approach by exacting an homage scarcely consistent with another's self-respect. The perfect simplicity of his character was reflected in the easiness of his carriage . . .'[15]

During these years, Thornwell's fame grew rapidly in both church and state. He was elected Moderator of the General Assembly of the (Old School) Presbyterian Church in the United States of America at the age of thirty-four; apparently the youngest man ever so honored. He attended most General Assemblies and addressed many important issues. He was looked upon as a fount of wisdom by many, though some – like the great Charles Hodge of Princeton – debated with him vigorously (as in the famous 1860 debate on Church Boards). Even those who disagreed with him acknowledged his gifts, as, for example, the famous Northern liberal minister, Henry Ward Beecher, who wrote after his death:

> . . . by common fame, Dr. Thornwell was the most brilliant minister in the Old School Presbyterian Church, and the most brilliant debater in the General Assembly. This reputation he early gained and never lost. Whenever he was present in the Assembly, he was always the first person pointed out to a stranger.[16]

Thornwell's remarkable abilities in debate flowed in large part from the brilliance of his intellect, with its unusual capacity to retain large amounts of material in several languages. He was usually careful not to display this capacity in public debate, but occasionally it evidenced itself. In 1857, the famous New England scholar and orator, Edward Everett, was in Columbia, South Carolina, and had a visit while there from Dr Thornwell.

> . . . the conversation turned upon the recurrence of certain ideas in different eras of the world. Mr. Everett illustrated it by reference to a passage in Thucydides, which he rendered into English. Dr. Thornwell replied by quoting, in the original Greek, a few lines from the same author. Mr. Everett rejoined once more in English, when Dr. Thornwell made a far more extended quotation from Thucydides, in the Greek. All were surprised and delighted at the exhibition of learning, so spontaneous as to be free from the suspicion of pedantry.[17]

With such a powerful mind, erudition and ethical interest, it is not surprising that Thornwell exercised strong moral influence in the counsels of state. The famous Southern senator, John C. Calhoun, highly respected Thornwell's grasp of political issues, and compared Thornwell to Timothy Dwight, his teacher at Yale.[18] Another famous congressional orator, Daniel Webster, after hearing a sermon by Thornwell in the South Carolina College Chapel said, '[it] was one of the finest exhibitions of pulpit eloquence I ever heard.'[19] In addition to educating many state leaders with a biblical world-and-life view, Thornwell influenced public opinion and public policy in the pre-war years by his widely-received and eloquent defense of the Southern understanding of domestic servitude (which, as we have briefly discussed in the introduction, was a very different approach from pagan forms of slavery). We can account for his opinions on this matter when we remember that, like all fallen human beings (even the redeemed), Thornwell was strongly influenced by the views of his culture, with the natural result that of course he had what later generations would see as glaring blind spots.

Thornwell was a very hard worker with continual demands upon his time, and did not have a robust physique. Hence he must have found it hard to practice the very advice he once gave to a younger minister: 'You will be able to accomplish more in the long run, by not overtasking yourself at the beginning . . .'[20] Thus, his friends, who valued so deeply his service to church, state and education, noticing that his physical condition was weakening, on two different occasions during his later years donated money to send him on trips to Europe. They hoped that the sea air and change of scenery would help restore his health. Dr Thornwell did enjoy these trips, in spite of frequent reference to homesickness in his letters. Much as he appreciated the sight-seeing, his greatest pleasure was meeting fellow scholars. He wrote the following about his time in Edinburgh (in 1860):

From Belfast I crossed the Channel to Glasgow, and then proceeded to Edinburgh, where I lingered for more than a week. The society there was truly refreshing. I was a great deal with the Principal of the New College, the Rev. Dr. Cunningham, an able and learned theologian; and spent part of a day very happily with Professor Fraser, the successor of Sir William Hamilton in the University of Edinburgh. I was gratified to find that I was not wholly unknown to the clergy of Scotland . . .'[21]

He also enjoyed discussions with Professor Mansel of Oxford University.

Thornwell's life work seemed to have reached its peak in his call in 1856 to be Professor of Didactic and Polemic Theology in Columbia Theological Seminary. Of this significant move, he wrote:

. . . I now perceive that all my training, whether moral, intellectual or spiritual, the bent of my studies, the peculiar turn of my mind, my cherished tastes and my chosen speculations, have all been controlled and modified and shaped with reference to the solemnities of this hour. God had this night in His own eternal view when in yonder college walls I rose up early and sat up late to store my mind with that knowledge which I then designed to make only an instrument of ambition.[22]

Thornwell filled this post with brilliant distinction; he continued to be an outstanding preacher, teacher, writer, theologian, educator, ecclesiastical statesman, venerated public figure and devoted husband and father. He never allowed the constant press of public demands and professional duties to cause him to neglect his primary responsibility to his own household. Whenever he was away from home, or whenever his children were away, he wrote them frequent and affectionate letters. These remarks to his daughter, Pattie, in 1860, are typical of his familial letters: '. . . I cannot spend the time more pleasantly than in conversing with the dear ones at home. Your mother and the children are never out of my mind. I think of you by day, and dream of you by night . . .'[23]

He faithfully and tactfully dealt with his children about their need of a personal, saving knowledge of Jesus Christ in his letters to them. These tender words to his son, Gillespie, then aged 15, in the year 1859, reflect the continual concern of one who was not only a famous theologian, but also a loving father:

. . . I have endeavored to commit you all to God; and there is nothing on which my heart is so much set as to see you all enlisted in the service of the Lord Jesus Christ. My cup of earthly happiness would be full, if you, and Jimmie, and Charlie, were only true Christians. You would then be safe for time and eternity. Depend upon it, my dear son, you will never repent of it, if you should now give your heart unto the Lord. Let me beg you to seek, this summer, the salvation of your soul. You will have time to think, and read, and pray. Write to me that you are not neglecting the one thing needful.'[24]

One of the sorest trials of his family life was the sudden illness and death of his eldest daughter, Nannie Witherspoon, who was just twenty years of age, and engaged to be married. When Thornwell returned home from the General Assembly of the Presbyterian Church in Indianapolis, he was shocked to find his beloved daughter in the throes of her final illness, on the very eve of her marriage. In fact, her father had hurried back in order to officiate at the wedding, to which the invitations had already been mailed.

In the progress of her disease, he wrestled with his grief, and could not easily give her up. When it became apparent that she must die, he took his wife into the adjoining room, and there the two knelt and prayed for help and for submission. At intervals, he read and prayed with the departing one; and she, in the triumph of her faith, became his comforter, and sought with tender words to reconcile him to the inevitable separation. It was a beautiful scene: this reversal of positions between the dying child and the strong father, writhing in the crucifixion of his affections. But, like David, when the blow fell, his prayer for help was answered, and he bowed himself, and said, 'It is the Lord!'[25]

His daughter said that she was just as willing to go into the arms of her Redeemer as into those of her husband, and she was buried in her wedding dress. 'Just a little after the day when she should have plighted her vows before the altar, the very attendants who, in a different scene, should have "rejoiced, hearing the bridegroom's voice," with their white gloves lifted the bier, and bore it to the grave.'[26]

It seemed appropriate that a public figure who was so devoted to his own wife and children should have an orphanage named in his honor soon after his death. The Thornwell Orphanage was founded in Clinton, South Carolina, in 1875, by one of his former students, the Rev. William Plumer Jacobs, who graduated from Columbia Seminary in 1864. Dr Jacobs was himself an orphan, and had been greatly encouraged by Dr Thornwell's compassion for the young. 'This was the first orphanage in South Carolina not supported by taxation.'[27] This institution still continues its ministry to children in 1991.

In addition to being a devoted husband and father, Thornwell was also profoundly devoted to the cause of the South in general, and to his native South Carolina in particular. Unlike most of his South Carolina compatriots, however, who were eager for secession from the United States Federal Government, Thornwell hoped against hope that a split would not occur between the Northern and Southern states, until it was at last too late. When he returned from his last European tour in 1860, he was surprised to discover that events were in motion – beyond any possibility of recall – for South Carolina to secede from the Union. He accepted the situation as it was, and threw himself and all of his energies into what we now know was the lost cause of Southern independence.

The political division soon led to an ecclesiastical division, which was also very painful to this devoted churchman. Yet he had to accept this situation as well. Much as he regretted the split between the Northern and Southern sections of the Old School Presbyterian Church, he took a leading hand in organizing the Presbyterian Church in the Confederate States of America in 1861. Not surprisingly, it was to him, in his capacity as the respected senior statesman, that the first General Assembly of the Confederate Presbyterian Church looked to write its explanatory letter, stating its reasons for withdrawal from its previous connection as well as its theological principles. This he did in the unanimously adopted document: 'The Address to all the Churches of Jesus Christ throughout the Earth.' In spite of his conviction that the Southern cause was right, and that the Southern Presbyterians had no choice but to leave the old denomination, Thornwell still was eager to do all he could to prevent bitterness and resentment against Christian brethren in the North. Thus, he attempted to have the First General Assembly of the Southern Church send an irenic Farewell Letter to the Northern Church from which they had just separated, but he was strongly voted down.

The national division between the states and within the church, and the Civil War that soon ensued, undoubtedly hastened Thornwell's early death at the age of forty-nine. His son, Gillespie, serving in the Confederate army, was wounded in battle in Virginia by a sabre thrust. Surviving the battle, he returned home for a period of convalescence, but the very day that the father and son parted in Charlotte, North Carolina, Dr Thornwell went to bed with his final illness. Gillespie returned to the Confederate army, in whose service he would be killed in 1863, barely a year after his father's death, for in August of 1862, owing to consumption and chronic dysentery, Thornwell breathed his last in the home of a friend, William White of Charlotte. His wife arrived from Columbia just before the end and along with their good friend from South Carolina, Dr John Adger, Nancy Thornwell heard her husband's final words, which were of wonder and praise: 'Wonderful! Beautiful! Nothing but space! Expanse! Expanse! Expanse!'

7

MAJESTIC PREACHING: THEOLOGY AND PASSION

We must now consider the one activity of Thornwell's brief, arduous and energetic life which he considered to be central – far more important in his own eyes than his remarkable academic leadership, much as he was evidently suited to that profession. There are several contemporary descriptions of his preaching.

For example, Dr J. W. Alexander of New York (son of Archibald Alexander of Princeton and author of a famous nineteenth-century work on preaching) once wrote of one of Thornwell's sermons: 'His sermon was ill delivered, but nevertheless a model of what is rare, viz.: burning hot argument, logic in ignition, and glowing more and more to the end: it was *a memoriter* [from memory], and with terrific *contentio laterum* [developing his argument by means of an antithesis].'[28] Speaking of Thornwell's earlier ministry, another of his hearers wrote: 'Mr. Thornwell's sermons, from the commencement of his preaching, were profound, logical and eloquent.'[29] And, praising a sermon Thornwell had preached in 1843, Dr Nathaniel Hewitt of Connecticut, said: 'Howe, Owen and Robert Hall re-appear in him. The philosophical acumen of Howe, the gospel unction of Owen, and the rhetoric of Hall, unite in this discourse; and in my humble opinion, no sermon has been produced in our country . . . equal to it.'[30]

Dr Palmer, Thornwell's perceptive biographer, ably summarizes the remarkable attributes of Thornwell's preaching power in terms of three combined elements:

To understand Dr. Thornwell's power, these several elements must be combined; his powerful logic, his passionate emotion, his majestic style, of which it may be said, as of Lord Brougham, that 'he wielded the club of Hercules entwined with roses.'[31]

When we think of Girardeau's preaching, we think of his vivid word painting, colored by his rich, artistic imagination and energized by the depth of his feeling for and rapport with the congregation. Thornwell's preaching was less aesthetic. He placed the strongest emphasis on a clear presentation of powerful truth, with one logical step following another, building up to a majestic climax at the end. Palmer analyzed Thornwell's logical approach to preaching in the following manner:

From all that has been said of his logical proclivity and scholastic training, it may be rightly inferred that his preaching was addressed predominantly, though not exclusively, to the understanding. Looking upon man as a being of intelligence, and upon the truth as the instrument of sanctification, he caused that truth to knock at the door of the understanding until she was admitted and entertained. He had a sublime faith in God's ordained method of reaching the affections through the proclamation of His Word. Eschewing all effort to work upon the superficial emotions, or to play upon natural sympathies, he addressed himself in earnest to present the whole truth of God, and to discuss its fundamental principles before men.

His analytic power was fully displayed in the pulpit. The clear statement of a case is often one-half of the argument. Stripping his subject of all that was adventitious, he laid bare to the eye the single principle upon which it turned; so single and so bare, that the most untrained were compelled to see precisely what was to be elucidated. Then followed a course of argument, close, logical, clear, profound, bending forward to one conclusion, towards which the hearer was carried, with his will or against it, led captive in chains of logic that could nowhere be broken. When the truth had won its way, and the mind was brought into a state of complete submission, the argument was gathered up in its weighty and practical conclusions, and hurled upon the conscience, compelling either the confession of guilt upon the one hand, or a complete stultification of reason upon the other. These appeals to the heart were often fearful in their solemnity; all the more because based upon the previous assent of the understanding. They were not mere exhortation, but a judicial finding in the court of the hearer's own conscience.

The preacher stood there as an attorney from heaven to indict and prosecute the sinner. The pleading has been heard; the argument for his conviction has been concluded; and the sinner only hears the sentence of condemnation from its throne of judgment, echoing through all the chambers of the soul. It was upon this plan most of the discourses of this matchless preacher were formed. It mattered little whether the exposition was of law or grace; there was the same enforcement of eternal and immutable principles, and the same judicial finding of guilt and shame, whether the offense was against the one or the other.[32]

* * *

The description of Thornwell as 'a theological preacher' is most apt.[33] He constantly employs careful logical steps in his argumentation, but the theme of his presentation is always theological. His preaching, while soundly based on biblical truth, is in most cases not the same sort of close, grammatical, historico-literary searching out, interpreting and applying of the biblical text that one finds in B. B. Warfield, John Murray, or Martyn Lloyd-Jones. Nonetheless, his sermons are based on specific biblical texts, and he does humbly and faithfully interact with them, though perhaps more in a theological than strictly expository way. Be that as it may, the content of his preaching is solidly biblical, resting upon a deep understanding of those scriptural doctrines of grace rediscovered in the great sixteenth-century Reformation.

In his study of Thornwell, Dr Morton Smith has rightly pointed out that the doctrine of justification was central to Thornwell's theology.[34] This theme was also central to his preaching ministry. In a graduation sermon addressed to the senior students of the South Carolina College, Thornwell states:

The cross of Christ is the center of the Christian system. From it we are instructed in the character of our Judge, the malignity of sin, our present condition and the prospects which await us beyond the grave . . . His glory is here displayed with a luster in comparison with which all other manifestations of His name are as the feeble light of the stars . . . The cross became the center of universal attraction, displayed the perfections of Deity in singular and rare combination, and was the source at once of rapture to angels, of terror to the lost and of hope to men. The death of Christ is without doubt the sublimest event in the annals of time or the record of eternity.[35]

Most of Thornwell's printed sermons are contained in Volume II of his *Works*, and as one goes through this volume, one constantly finds Thornwell drawing attention to the profoundly significant connection between the substitutionary atonement of Christ and tremendous joy in the believer. In his two great sermons on 'The Necessity and Nature of Christianity' and 'The Necessity of the Atonement', he is at pains to point out the devastating consequences of false views of the death of Christ in removing any hope of peace and joy for needy souls. He says, for instance:

The glory of Christianity is its Savior, and his power to save is in the blood by which He extinguished the fires of the curse, and the righteousness by which He bought life for all His followers. Jesus made our curse, Jesus made our righteousness, this, this is the Gospel! All else is philosophy and vain deceit. This it is which gives Christianity its power. By this, and this alone, it subdues the ferocity of passion, disarms temptation of its violence, disrobes the world of its charms, changes the tiger into the lamb, and makes the lion eat straw like the ox. This constitutes the grand difference between the religion of Mohammed and the religion of Jesus, between the Koran and the Bible.[36]

Granted the overarching importance of atonement and justification by faith, we are not surprised to find throughout the preaching of Thornwell a continual call to conversion, and an instant urging to faith and repentance. In more modern terms, it might be called a pressing for decision – although (unlike some modern preachers) his imperative to trust Christ is always clearly grounded on the preliminary indicatives of the person and work of Christ. One has merely to read the last three or four pages of almost any of his sermons to see his emphasis on an appropriate response to the message. In a sermon on 'The Gospel Ministry,' Thornwell asks:

How can a minister who feels the value of the soul, or the realities of eternity, be cold and unmoved when warning sinners to flee from the wrath to come? Heaven or hell, life or death, eternal life or eternal death, depend on the success of his message, and can he be indifferent whether it is received or not? Can he see the terrible cloud of Divine wrath gathering thick above the sinner's head ready to beat in one tremendous storm upon him and not be in earnest in warning him of danger! Eternity is at stake! The minister must be earnest; if he has the soul and the feelings of a Christian he must be earnest. The law thunders in terrific peals its notes of condemnation; the Savior groans and dies and meets its demands; yet the sinner is asleep – asleep on the very brink of hell, and who will awake him? Sinai and Calvary alike urge the minister to be earnest; he must lift his voice like a trumpet until the sinner hears his warning and obeys his instructions.[37]

The note that Thornwell strikes here – as in so much of his preaching – needs to be heard among Christians today. It may well be the case that one of the reasons for the demise of the Presbyterian Church in the U.S. in this century was the absence of earnestness in beseeching men to be reconciled to God. It is hard to resolve the complex question of how the Southern church was lost to the forces of liberalism. Without attempting to list all of the possible reasons, it nevertheless does seem that at least one of the significant factors in the moving of our church from conservative to modernist theology was the lack of evangelistic urgency among ordinary pastors throughout the South.

For instance, when the present writer took up a preaching ministry in the Pee Dee area of South Carolina, a number of older Christians used to recall the lives and preaching of several of the older ministers who had served in that area from the First World War until the nineteen-fifties. If their reports are correct, these men were most certainly not theologically liberal, but rather it is clear that something had dropped out of their preaching. Somehow between the time of Dabney and Girardeau in the late 1890s and the generation of preachers who were active from the 1920s onwards, the element of earnest exhortation to conversion had seriously weakened, although of course it never entirely faded. During this time the absurd impression arose that the call for sinners to repent and believe the gospel was solely for Baptists or Pentecostals, and that the respectable Presbyterians had either graduated beyond such appeals, or could assume that covenant children were safe because of their connection with the organized church. Indeed, the Southern church has not yet recovered from this woeful misconception.

In this connection, it is very moving to read, in Palmer's biography of Thornwell, of the way in which this profound covenant theologian wrote letters to his own children urging them to cast themselves on the mercy of the Lord Jesus Christ. He wanted them to be sure that they had specifically repented of their sins and had a saving interest in the only Redeemer of God's elect. As another example of his evangelistic concern, listen to Thornwell's sermon on 'The Priesthood of Christ' to the young men of South Carolina College:

It is my earnest desire and prayer that those who hear me may be saved. The solicitude which I always feel for the young men of my charge is collected to its greatest intensity when they are about to be dismissed from my pastoral instruction and care. If it could avail, I could weep tears of blood over those who have never been persuaded to become reconciled to God . . . when I reflect that they are probably hearing my voice for the last time, I am constrained to cry aloud in one final, desperate effort to dispel the enchantment which, if not dispelled, must seal them up in death.[38]

At the same time, it is important for us to realize that Thornwell's earnest and tender calls for conversion were solidly based upon a well-balanced understanding of the scriptural order of salvation. He continually emphasizes the priority of the sovereign and gracious God in his free election of sinners to be awakened from their death-like slumbers so that they may place their trust in him. Thornwell's preaching has in common with his fellow Calvinists, Girardeau, Palmer and Baker, the frequent teaching of the scriptural order of salvation. Unlike some today who are afraid that a robust Calvinism will turn sinners away, and so become Arminian in their methods (and in their message – by leaving some important truths unsaid), these fathers of Southern Calvinism regularly and enthusiastically taught the facts of redemption from a God-centered perspective – and saw thousands converted.[39]

Another important emphasis in the content of Thornwell's preaching, and a theme which underlies the whole necessity of atonement and justification, is his clarion proclamation of the holiness and glory of God. He has some moving passages on the filial devotion of Jesus to the holiness of the Father as manifested in his willing self-sacrifice to preserve and demonstrate the unsullied honor of God in the salvation of sinners.[40]

Dr William Childs Robinson, one of the twentieth-century successors of Thornwell at Columbia Seminary, suggested with great insight that Thornwell saw the essence of sin to be a refusal to depend on God as Father.[41] With his God-centered approach, which anchors the meaning of human existence in the heart of the heavenly Father, it is not surprising that he has much to say about the connection of holiness and true joy.[42] His justly famous 'Discourses on Truth' (which were appreciated by the great Professor of Scottish Common Sense Philosophy in Edinburgh, Sir William Hamilton) are lectures which examine and then apply the doctrine of the holiness of God to the major ethical responsibilities of human life. In the tradition of John Calvin and of the best scriptural theologians, Thornwell always views the activities and final goal of human life under the rubric of the glory of God. This is a regular emphasis of all his preaching: God's glory is always the first priority and the final justification for all that is to be thought, said and done.

Another great theme of Thornwell's preaching was his insistence that we must know God directly; that Christianity is not primarily a philosophy or code of ethics but 'the life of God in the soul of man'. Often this was his emphasis in sermons against the various forms of Deism which had invaded the intellectual centers of America from more liberal Europe. In the mold of the Apostles John and Paul, Augustine, John Calvin and John Owen, not to mention a host of others, Thornwell shows that genuine Christianity is a life in the Spirit, a direct experience of 'Christ in you the hope of glory'. He decries the polite, fastidious intellectual form of religion which would keep God at arm's length from one's own life. Listen to Thornwell on 'The Personality of the Holy Ghost':

> Such is the deplorable skepticism which prevails, especially among those who claim to be of the better sort, upon the whole subject of Divine influences, that many are afraid to expect them, others despise them . . . he who professes to believe by a divine power, to see the truth in a divine light, and to relish its beauty with a divine affection – will be mocked as an enthusiast and denounced as a visionary . . . Now, if it should be found that those who are despised as rabid fanatics are really the children of God, and that what are regarded as their dreams of folly are really the suggestions of the Holy Ghost, the fastidious skeptics who denounce them would be involved in as awful

a sin as the haughty Pharisees who ascribed our Savior's miracles to the finger of Beelzebub.[43]

Later in the same sermon, Thornwell makes the point that truly knowing God is more than an assent to correct propositions (though certainly it includes that); rather, it is a direct, inner experience of his life within our life. He says:

We may in words profess to receive the operations of the Spirit, but it is only an empty declaration if we do not feel that influences have been exerted on us – our own hearts, understandings and consciences – that could not possibly have been effected without the agency of a glorious and extraordinary Person. We must have experimental evidence, the witness within ourselves, that the Author of our faith, our hopes and our joys is a living Person, abundant in goodness, rich in grace and unlimited in knowledge.

Such are the relations of the Spirit to the understandings and consciences of men in applying the great salvation of the Gospel that it seems to be impossible that His office should ever be discharged in the mind of a sinner without producing a consciousness of the extraordinary change which has been effected . . Wherever He dwells there must be displays of His glory and power.[44]

Yet at the same time, balanced theologian that he is, Thornwell carefully safeguards against what we would today call Charismatic excesses, which lay claim to communications or even revelations of the Spirit apart from and unconnected to the written Word. He clearly distinguishes between illumination and inspiration:

I do not mean to insinuate, however, that the divine illumination which is the only cause of supernatural faith is, by any means, identical with prophetic inspiration. There is certainly a vast difference betwixt imparting original revelations, and enabling the understanding to perceive the impressions of divine glory in a revelation communicated. But He who, in the one case, can manifest His presence so as to silence doubt and generate conviction, can also do it in the other.[45]

Closely connected to his emphasis on the direct knowledge of God in a true salvation experience and the continuing Christian life, he preached against the kind of superficially correct Christianity which he saw invading the mid-nineteenth-century, professedly Calvinist churches of America.[46] Though committed to giving a powerful 'reason for the hope that was within him', he also preached against a false, man-centered confidence in a type of nominalistic apologetics, which implied that by human manipulation of clever words and arguments, one could accomplish the work of God as it were without God.[47]

As we summarize the content of Thornwell's preaching, we may well believe that his logic was on fire because he was in direct contact with the living God who is a consuming fire. God used his preaching to bring congregations into touch with the purging, transforming reality of his own divine presence.

* * *

Important as the divine element is in the preaching of Thornwell, it certainly does not preclude us from taking a look at the more human side of his pulpit work. Palmer tells us that in Thornwell's earlier days he preached for only thirty minutes, but in later life tended to preach for 'the more orthodox' (in nineteenth-century terms) sixty minutes.[48] Thornwell's sermons are generally clearly outlined, though often the outline is more natural than obtrusive. His sermons have the great value of progressive thought in their various stages, which with each part gather momentum, and increase the forcefulness of the message as they approach the climax. The result is that the logical presentation of the truth operates as a mighty hand moving closer and closer to the will of the hearer.

Thornwell usually handles the context of the passage fairly,[49] allows the precisions of the grammar to instruct his interpretation,[50] and knows how to put questions to the text which permit the text to reveal its truth to the questioner.[51] Unlike some who think expository preaching is merely paraphrasing the Bible with some application added on at the end, Thornwell grapples with the complexities, depths and interconnections of the text; he questions the text and lets the text question him. It is this insight into the interconnections of the truth of God which Palmer isolates as one of the major aspects of Thornwell's preaching:

> . . . the power he possessed of sometimes illuminating the whole gospel in a single discourse. We enter, for example, a chamber at twilight; and, with a dim, uncertain vision, recognize the furniture

and appointments. Each object is disclosed, but in faint outline; and the relation of the parts to each other can be but imperfectly traced. Suddenly a taper is applied to a single burner, and one jet of flame is sufficient to light up the whole . . .

Just so, the truths to which we have been listening all our lives are disposed in a certain catechetical order in our mind, yet fragmentary and disjointed . . . His power of analysis stripped every subject of all that was adventitious or collateral . . . With this ultimate principle in the grasp, the hearer had the key to unlock the entire subject . . . As every system, too, however complex, must hang upon a few cardinal postulates, it was his delight to seize upon those which were fundamental in Christianity, and, with amazing constructive skill, build up the grand temple before the eyes of the audience, laying beam upon beam, and stone upon stone, and 'bringing forth the headstone thereof, with shoutings of, Grace grace unto it.'[52]

* * *

It was his burden and joy not only to convey his vision of the profound interconnections of gospel truth to congregations, but also to instruct those who would be future preachers to the people of God. He wished to make clear to them how they could accomplish this task, without of course denying the centrality of divine assistance. Thornwell, in company with all historic Presbyterians, believed in a well-educated ministry, specifically so that the Word of God could be faithfully handled. He gives some interesting advice to aspiring preachers about this matter of knowledge. His advice is in sharp contrast to modern assertions that computer technology will change the shape of education by placing vast amounts of information at our fingertips and thus precluding the need for memorization. Thornwell would be rightly appalled by such a suggestion! On the contrary, he insists that a well-equipped preacher must have his learning in his head: 'So the minister is to be fully furnished for the wants of his age with things new and old – a copious variety of learning – and the storehouse must be his mind and not his library, his head and not his shelves.'[53]

In addition to wide learning, personally assimilated and ever ready for kingdom usage, Thornwell believed that young preachers should consciously seek to be eloquent in their command of language – in order all the more effectively to harness language to the good of souls and the glory of God. Palmer says:

> . . . it was his habit before any great public effort, to tone his style by reading a few pages from some master in composition. Sometimes it was a passage from Robert Hall, sometimes from Edward Gibbon, sometimes of Edmund Burke, sometimes of glorious old Milton . . . His spoken style was, however, unquestionably the result of his life's study. His habits of close thinking exacted a choice of words.[54]

And Thornwell warmly recommended this practice to aspiring preachers.

However, of much greater importance than fine use of language was his fervent exhortation to all true gospel preachers never to be merely perfunctory in their preaching; never to go through the motions merely out of duty or desire to avoid shame.[55] Rather, he urged them constantly to seek the illumination of the Holy Spirit, his unction, his blessing, and – as was so amply illustrated by the sermons of this master preacher himself – to seek the fire of the altar to fall on the offering of their preaching.[56]

If this be our desire and our practice today, then we too, like Thornwell, will find all along the years of our preaching that God's Word is like a fire and a hammer to accomplish all the work that God has chosen us from eternity to accomplish in his power. May it be so!

PART THREE

BENJAMIN MORGAN PALMER: CAPTURING THE HEART OF NEW ORLEANS

8

PALMER'S FORMATIVE YEARS IN SOUTH CAROLINA

The preaching ministry of the great Southern Presbyterian orator and pastor, B. M. Palmer, may be best described by referring to pictures of God's blessings on his Old Testament people. He was not unlike the prophet Elisha, whose life conveyed healing and restoration to many in his generation. Or we could characterize his ministry in the pulpit as that of pouring the healing 'balm of Gilead', of which the prophet Jeremiah speaks in two places, into wounded, hurting lives. Palmer himself tells us in one of his sermons that he would like 'to pour in a drop of balm'. That chance remark effectively brings into focus for us, both the attitude of his heart and the effects of his preaching and pastoral work.[1]

Much of Palmer's ministerial life was during times of war and the so-called 'Reconstruction' following the War Between the States. As a result, he lived and ministered at a time when there was widespread financial loss, epidemic and plague. But it was also a period of an increasing secularism in the prevailing culture, coupled with growing liberal tendencies in many American churches. In a word, the multitudes among whom he walked lived in times of distress and were made up of people who were in great need of healing and restoration. By the grace of God, Palmer was one who was supremely equipped to meet such a need. To read his sermons – even ninety years later or more – is to sense a healing hand massaging balm into our own troubled spirits.

Palmer was born on January 25, 1818, in Charleston, South Carolina, into a well-known ministerial family which was originally of New England Puritan stock. However, the family had been very much a part of the Southern scene for the previous three generations, and throughout his life, even after the nearly fifty years he later spent in New Orleans, Palmer would often say, 'I am a South Carolinian, you know'.[2] As a child, he lived for several years in Walterboro, S.C., which had been founded as a sort of summer retreat for a number of the leading plantation families of the surrounding Low Country. Here he was exposed to a community of cultured, well-educated people, who served as an intellectual and moral stimulus. His mother also effectively stimulated his linguistic and educational advancement by reading to him, 'besides the Bible, all of Shakespeare's plays, Scott's novels, and Milton's *Paradise Lost*,'[3] and also exposing him to the writings of John Locke.

Although he belonged to a widely respected family, young Palmer was not brought up in affluent circumstances, for his father was a poorly paid rural pastor all the days of his long life of more than ninety years. Yet it is clear that Edward Palmer and his wife, Sarah, gladly sacrificed to provide the best possible education for their children. In his early teens, Palmer was sent to Amherst, Massachusetts, for his college education. While he did receive a solid classical grounding there, the experience was not a particularly happy one for him: he was a South Carolinian in a Northern environment at a time when strong feelings were being incited against the South because of the Abolitionist movement and the Nullification controversy. As a result, he decided to leave Amherst abruptly, without taking the time to seek the advice of his parents. This so strained the relationship with his father that for some time he was not even inclined to speak to his son when he returned to the family home in Colleton County, South Carolina. Although Mrs Sarah Palmer was sympathetic with the viewpoints of both her husband and her son, and worked hard to repair the relationship, it took some two or three years to heal the rupture. Meanwhile, therefore, young Palmer left the tense atmosphere of home and taught for the next two or three years in village schools in McPhersonville and then in Mt Pleasant, near Charleston.

Later, he wrote about his attitude to life at that period, when he was as yet unconverted, and chafing under a certain bitterness owing to his negative experiences at Amherst:

I was irreligious, nay, worse than that I was hostile to religion, in decided hostility to God and the Gospel, in such evil posture that, had I fallen into the hands of scoffers I might have become as infidel as they. Surrounded by companions as unrestrained as myself, most of whom sank into premature graves, through the mercy of God I was saved.[4]

Then in 1836, at the age of eighteen, the great change came:

. . . he was led to accept Christ and unite with the church through the personal work of a cousin, Rev. I. S. K. Axson, afterward Dr. Axson of the Independent Presbyterian Church of Savannah, Georgia. Very tenderly he said to young Palmer as he bade him good night in his room: 'My cousin, you are growing up fast to manhood; is it not a good time to give yourself to the Savior, when you are soon to choose the course in life which you shall pursue?' And Palmer adds in writing of the incident: 'Before reaching the door of his chamber, I took the solemn vow that I would make the salvation of my soul the supreme business of my life.' And though it was months before peace came, when it came, he adds, 'it came to stay, and through five and fifty years it has deepened in the soul to which it came as the balm of heaven.'[5]

He then attended the University of Georgia, graduating at the head of his class. At first he hesitated between law and ministry, but soon decided to prepare for the gospel ministry by studying at Columbia Theological Seminary, from 1839 to 1841. Probably the greatest influence on Palmer during those years was not his seminary professors, but James H. Thornwell. He first knew Thornwell as a professor at South Carolina College, and then, after 1840, as pastor and preacher of First Presbyterian Church of Columbia. They became close personal friends, and Palmer would later write Thornwell's biography.

Thomas Cary Johnson, the biographer of both Robert L. Dabney and Benjamin M. Palmer, traced the considerable influence of Thornwell upon Palmer:

There can be no question that there were great differences between the mental constitutions of these two men. Palmer excelled in his capacities as a word painter and in dealing with the sentimental and pathetic; Thornwell in the power of reasoning, and speculative thought. But there can be as little question that they were enough alike for Thornwell to mold Palmer to a considerable degree. To this influence is, perhaps, to be traced the theological type of his preaching that prevailed far along in his life . . . Thornwell unconsciously became, unawares it may be to Palmer, his model, yet in no cramping way. Palmer's individuality was too strong to follow Thornwell in aught else than what met his judgment's approval.[6]

After graduation, Palmer served at first as minister of the Presbyterian church in Anderson, South Carolina, then in Savannah, Georgia, until 1843, when he was called to replace Thornwell as pastor of First Presbyterian Church of Columbia. For the next eleven years Palmer served as minister of this church, while his friend, Thornwell, served as President of South Carolina College. The Calvinist influence in the state capital of South Carolina was thus remarkably strong during those pre-war years, and all during this time Palmer's preaching abilities greatly increased and his fame began to spread abroad.

Palmer's increasing fame was based neither on his personal appearance nor on a wealthy familial background. He was far from handsome and his parents were far from rich. According to his biographer:

Benjamin Morgan Palmer was under, rather than over, medium height, slight in build, though deep in the chest . . . His head was small . . . His forehead, however, was relatively ample. His eyes were very fine, dark brown, sparkling and brilliant. His mouth was not handsome, but of generous proportions, the most conspicuous feature of his face, suggestive of sweetness and eloquence and strength . . .[7]

Yet his contemporaries also noted that, though lacking physical beauty, his bodily movements were graceful, his general bearing was dignified, and that he exhibited 'an utter freedom from self-consciousness.'[8] Most important of all, his character and eloquence fully overcame any lack of physical attractiveness.

His Christian character and sermonic eloquence also overcame his relatively poor background. Palmer's lack of financial endowment at first caused his future father-in-law, Professor

George Howe of Columbia Seminary (Palmer's own teacher at that time), to oppose the seminarian's proposed marriage to his step-daughter, Mary Augusta McConnell. Palmer, however, was not easily dissuaded and persisted. Shortly after he graduated from Columbia Seminary and entered the pastorate in Savannah, his old professor at last consented to the marriage. Over the years, Palmer's relationship to his parents-in-law was a very cordial one, with great respect and devotion on both sides.

Many years later, when Palmer was the famous preacher and substantial citizen of New Orleans, it was much to his credit that he gladly consented to his daughter Gussie's marriage to a young man who had very slender financial resources. As Dr Palmer wrote at that time to his sister: 'She marries a poor man, who has not the leisure nor the means even for a bridal trip – or I would send them on to you. But God often makes the poor rich in the smallness of their desires – and it is so with them. Mr. Colcock is a young man of excellent points; and will, I hope, make her happy. If a woman's *heart* be satisfied, that is the *all*.'[9] Palmer had not forgotten his own background.

Palmer had a distinguished stage on which to develop his remarkable abilities and consecration during his years in Columbia, from 1843 to 1855. The First Presbyterian Church 'embraced many families of commanding position and influence in the capital city', and Dr Thornwell himself was one of Palmer's regular auditors in the congregation.[10] 'The members of the State Legislature, and of the courts of justice, the student bodies of the State College and of Columbia Theological Seminary, during their respective term times, presented severally great opportunities for a wide, pervasive and exceptionally potent influence.'[11] He began his ministry there on January 29, 1843, with an exposition of the words of Balaam in Numbers 22:38: 'And Balaam said unto Balak, Lo, I am come unto thee: have I now any power at all to say any thing? the word that God putteth in my mouth, that shall I speak.' Palmer developed his text by way of two propositions:

1. That true ministers of the gospel are specially called to their office by God himself, and their fields of labor specially designated.
2. That all true ministerial ability and authority are derived from God.

Having argued these propositions in a very able manner, the preacher

closed by reflecting upon the great practical importance of his theme, which reveals to us:
(1) The relation which the gospel minister sustains to God; (2) the relation which he sustains to his people; and (3) the source whence he should desire his encouragement.[12]

Thomas Cary Johnson summarized the young preacher's points as follows:

In Mr. Palmer's view the minister of the Gospel is 'a messenger from God to speak only the word that is put into his mouth.' He may 'not invent or add anything to the message. His sole care must be to inquire what God the Lord will say.' Touching his relation to the people, Mr. Palmer holds, that 'the pastoral commission is no contract formed merely for the pleasure and amusement of the hearers. The pastor is not called upon to cater to the various tastes which may perchance prevail among his auditors. His duty is to study God's Book, to expound its doctrines, to enforce its precepts, to urge its motives, to present its promises, to recite its warnings, to declare its judgments.' In fine, the minister is to look for his encouragement to God rather than to man.[13]

As Palmer's biographer notes, this inaugural sermon '. . . was prophetic of the character of his teaching throughout the Columbia pastorate and to the end of his life.'[14] Unfortunately, practically none of his Columbia preaching was published, although much of it is apparently still extant in manuscript form. His biographer lists nearly two pages' worth of sermon titles from this period, dealing with topics such as: 'The Amount of Moral Evidence in Support of Christianity,' 'The Father Glorified by the Son,' 'The Gospel, the Power of God,' 'Christ in Us,' 'Mortification of Sin,' 'Practical Uses of Predestination,' 'Future Punishment,' 'God not the Author of Sin,' 'The Soul Lost by Attending to Trifles,' 'The Covenant with Adam,' 'Duty of Family Instruction,' and 'Infant Baptism Warranted by the Church Charter.' One feature that we notice in the long list of Columbia sermon titles is wide variety – a salient characteristic of his preaching to the end. Although he was considered 'a born speaker', it was clear to the congregation that 'his skill in handling themes and audiences grew with the months. He possessed a growing faculty of clear explication, popular but accurate statement of points, luminous and noble illustrations.'[15]

But Benjamin Palmer was not only developing his preaching abilities, he was also maturing as an individual Christian and as a pastor. In later life, for example, he felt that he had acted rashly at times during his early years – in Savannah even more so than in Columbia. On one occasion before a prayer meeting in Savannah, a rather shy church member privately requested Palmer not to call on him to pray. However, once the prayer meeting started, the young minister immediately called on this very man to pray! After calling upon him yet again, and meeting with silence, Palmer stated: 'Brother ———, we shall just sit here till you lead us in prayer.' The timid gentleman then complied. Palmer later regretted his action, and as an elderly man was asked if he would act in this way again. He smiled and said: 'No, I think that is a case of God's overruling the rashness of my youth for good. Had the circumstances of God's ordering been different, my rashness might have been followed by much evil.'[16]

Recollections of the Columbia period written some forty years later give us insight into another means that God used then to mature, deepen and sweeten his servant. In his book *The Broken Home or Lessons in Sorrow*, he recounts how during this time, he and his wife had been blessed with the birth of their first child, an attractive, blond-headed son. All seemed to be well until the little boy was about twenty months old. Then he became diseased. His father describes what happened:

> . . . the earthly blight . . . shrivelled up the little form, until the loose flesh lapped over the thin bones like an unfitting garment. The hunger of disease could find nothing for its insatiate voracity, but the juices of the body on which it fed; and the breathing skeleton lay at length upon a pillow on the mother's lap. How old the child grew in two short months and how tall its little limbs became! Every trace of infantile beauty was effaced, only the golden curls floated over the pale brow; and the brilliant eyes which strangers in the street stooped to gaze upon, burned now with a feverish luster.[17]

Palmer relates something of the agony he passed through as he kept watch by the bed of his dying son. He speaks of how he grieved and interceded for strength to submit to God's will, and of how the hope of the Covenant of Grace which was witnessed to in the child's baptism at last broke through the gloom:

Days were spent in wrestling intercession – days which were darkened with awe under a sense of this fearful trust; until at length a peace broke upon the soul, like the peace which first lifted the burden of sin in his own conversion. A blessed token was enjoyed that his prayers had gone up as a memorial before God; and he sat beside his dying boy with the strong comfort of believing that the promise of the covenant was assured to his seed forever.[18]

For the rest of his life, Benjamin Palmer would be God's instrument of comfort to the grieving. In the words of St Paul, he would now be able '. . . to comfort them which are in any trouble with the comfort by which he himself was comforted of God' (2 Cor. 1:4). And in his later ministry, this man, whose unique characteristic turned out to be his ability to apply the balm of Gilead to the wounded soul, would learn many another lesson in both sorrow and comfort.

His time at the First Presbyterian Church of Columbia ended in 1854, when the synod of South Carolina called him to serve as Professor of Ecclesiastical History in the seminary in that city, but he remained there only two years, for he felt that his heart lay in the pastorate rather than in teaching. Professor W. T. Hall, who taught for many years at Columbia Seminary, sat as a student under Palmer's teaching in 1855–56. Hall later wrote that Palmer was the best teacher the students had until Thornwell arrived, and that if Palmer had chosen to devote his life to teaching, 'he would have made a great reputation and have been a pillar in the Seminary.'[19] Indeed, during this time Palmer was offered a Chair at Princeton Seminary.

To run ahead in our story, although Palmer would soon leave Columbia for over a half century's ministry in New Orleans, he did return to both the Columbia Seminary and First Presbyterian Church, when he had to evacuate New Orleans after its capture by Federal forces during the War Between the States. Thus during the 1863–64 academic session, Palmer taught once again in the seminary. This time he taught not church history, but systematic theology in order to fill the sad vacancy left by the death of Dr Thornwell. The curriculum that Palmer followed during that time tells us something not only about his professorate, but also about the theology underlying his long years of doctrinal preaching. He describes it in his own words:

The leading text-book has been the 'Institutes' of Calvin – the students being required to examine, in connection with it, the works of Turretin, of Principal Hill, and of Dick, – and the free use also of Hodge's 'Outlines of Theology,' . . . The manuscript lectures of Dr. Thornwell being fortunately in my possession have also been read to the classes, and enlarged upon in oral explanation.[20]

9

HOW ELOQUENCE AND COMPASSION MOVED A CITY

Though not lacking ability as a teacher, Palmer felt called to the parish ministry. Thus, in 1856 he entered upon what would be the great work of his lifetime: the pastorate of the First Presbyterian Church of New Orleans, Louisiana. He would remain here until his death in 1902, with the exception of the war years, when he returned to South Carolina. Palmer's influence in New Orleans, and beyond, was immense, growing and spreading for nearly half a century. Generally, more than 1,500 people filled the large church to hear him preach on Sabbath days. For two years his sermons were printed weekly by a local newspaper, and were yearly bound and distributed, rather like those of his great contemporary, Charles H. Spurgeon in London.[21] He was considered to be a model preacher both in America and beyond. People who heard Palmer preach believed that his excellent voice greatly increased the sway he exercised over audiences. In this he was blessed by nature with a throat of silver and a tongue of gold, like George Whitefield a century before him, and John L. Girardeau in his own generation.

His organs of speech were his greatest physical endowments for the function of preaching. His voice was 'wonderful,' indefinitely flexible and of great compass, adapting itself to the size of the audience room . . . always musical, even when thundering denunciations against sin and wrong, and often as sweet as a mother's lullaby . . . As he had the power by the choice of his words, of calling up before the mind pictures . . . so he had the power of expressing every emotion in his voice. His voice thrilled with joy, was swathed with woe, pulsated with hope, wailed with despair . . . Some of (his congregation) say that he never shed a tear in the pulpit, so perfect was his self-control, and that 'all his tears were in his voice' . . .[22]

He was also one of the pillars of the church as a whole. In the excitement following the Southern firing upon Fort Sumter which set off the War for Southern Independence, the Gardiner-Spring Resolution was passed by his denomination, requiring allegiance to the Federal (Northern) Government. Thus the Presbyterians of the South were forced to leave the Old School Presbyterian Church. It was Palmer who preached the opening sermon at the first General Assembly of the Confederate Presbyterian Church, when it was organized in 1861 in Augusta, Georgia, and he was elected its first moderator. In later years he continued to serve as a very conservative force in the denomination. On one occasion, he even alleged that Robert L. Dabney had taken the liberal side on a certain ecclesiastical question! So solidly conservative was he, that in the early 1870s he seriously considered whether it would be necessary to leave the Southern Presbyterian Church in which he felt he could trace dangerous broadening and liberalizing tendencies.[23]

Palmer had strong influence not only in church, but also in society and the state. Although he was an adherent of the doctrine of 'the spirituality of the church' (which precludes the church from directly interfering in civil affairs), he had been an open and eloquent proponent of Southern secession. He preached a famous (and to some, notorious) Thanksgiving Day Sermon in 1860 in New Orleans, which essentially called for separation from the Northern states. Many contemporary observers – even in other denominations – believed that this sermon was influential in encouraging the civil officials of the state of Louisiana (who were then hesitating on the question) to decide for secession.[24] There is no doubt that in the years prior to the end of the Civil War, Palmer did believe that the civil government 'should acknowledge Christ as God of Providence.'[25] And while he avoided direct pulpit discussion of societal issues for nearly all his long ministry, he was largely responsible for purging Louisiana of the corrupt lottery system in the early 1890s.

He also took a strong public stand in favor of the Jews when they were being persecuted in Eastern Europe in the late nineteenth century. For example, in response to Russian persecution of the Jews, Dr Palmer attended a public meeting in New Orleans in 1882, and was one of the main speakers, along with Jewish rabbis and other distinguished leaders. He even helped make plans to offer a home to the persecuted in New Orleans, closing his speech with two sentences that are said to have caused his audience, which included numerous Jews, to go wild with applause: 'Whenever persecution bursts upon the Jew there would I be at his side – an Hebrew of the Hebrews – to suffer and to do. If we cannot stay the hand of persecution abroad, let us welcome them to our homes and our bosoms here . . .'[26]

Palmer in Louisiana was in many respects much like Robert McCheyne, the Bonars and others in the mid-nineteenth-century Church of Scotland, who had a great love for the Jews and were active in seeking to win them for the Lord. What the Jews of New Orleans thought of him was illustrated in a 'chance happening' in the later years of his life:

> While in New York, during the winter of 1896 to 1897, Miss Agnes McMaster, of Columbia, S.C., struck with the voice of a young shop woman, said to her, 'You are not a Northerner?' 'No,' was the reply, 'I am from New Orleans.' 'I do not know anyone in New Orleans but Dr. Palmer,' next remarked the purchaser. 'Why,' exclaimed the saleswoman, 'I am an Israelite and we do not let the Presbyterians claim Dr. Palmer; we all claim him.' And her face beamed with delight.[27]

And when his old friends, the McMaster family of Columbia, wrote him about this meeting with the Jewess in New York, Dr Palmer replied in terms reminiscent of 'The Puritan Hope' (to borrow the title of the 1970 work by Iain H. Murray on this subject):

> . . . the Jews here seem to regard me in the light of a special friend. They do not, however, know the secret of this, which is the prophetic announcement of their being gathered at last into the Redeemer's Church . . . The Savior will have his triumph at last, even from those who have rejected him for centuries. We can all, therefore, by anticipating join in the words we so often sing:

'Joy to the world, the Lord is come,
Let earth receive her King.'[28]

We would be seriously mistaken, however, to think of Palmer primarily as a social activist or a moral or political controversialist. The considerable influence which he wielded in society and state came from his never-ceasing motivation to administer the healing balm of the gospel to a generation blighted with the multifarious effects of the sickness of sin. He may well have been mistaken in some of the actions he took in relation to the burning questions of his day, but the source of his motivation, as a debtor to Jew and Gentile, was his desire to see the healing hand of the Good Shepherd laid on the multitudes for whom he felt responsible (cf. Romans 1:14 and 9:3).

This central motivation of Palmer's life is illustrated in self-sacrificial actions during perilous circumstances in both New Orleans and Columbia. In 1858 the pestilence of yellow fever struck New Orleans, and large numbers of people left the city. While this included many pastors who abandoned their flocks, Dr Palmer remained in order to visit the sick and dying, and in the words of his biographer, 'to offer the consolation of the Gospel, and any other service which it was in his power to give . . .'[29] During that year, some 4,858 people in the city died of the fever and Palmer not only visited his own people, but others, particularly those who had no pastor. 'Indeed, it was his custom, while on his beneficent rounds, ministering to his own people, to enter every house on the way which displayed the sign of fever within; to make his way quietly to the sick room, utter a prayer, offer the consolation of the Gospel, and any other service which it was in his power to give; and then as quietly to leave.'[30]

Twenty years later, in 1878, Palmer was equally faithful and active in visiting those who were once again struck down by another outbreak of yellow fever. Increasing age had not affected his activity in the least. He wrote to his sister, Mrs Edgeworth Bird, the following report on his pastoral work at that time: 'You will form some idea of the trial, when I state that during three months, I paid each day from thirty to fifty visits, praying at the bedside of the sick, comforting the bereaved, and burying the dead; and that, too, without intermitting the worship of the Sabbath or even the prayer meeting in the week.'[31] Such actions prompted a famous Jewish rabbi of New Orleans to observe, 'It was thus that Palmer got the heart as well as the ear of New Orleans. Men could not resist one who gave himself to such ministry as this.'[32]

A committee of the New Orleans Presbytery stated in 1903, a year after Palmer's death, that for both preaching and pastoral compassion:

> . . . He was without a peer, preaching, praying, guiding the inquiring soul, ministering to the dying, bearing them, as it were, into the very presence of the gracious Savior, comforting the sorrowing, taking them upon his own great heart, discovering to them the heart of the sympathizing Lord. Into how many homes of his people, of our people, of us his brethren in the ministry, has he entered in times of grief, 'the Son of Consolation'! Throughout the community, throughout the land, there are thousands who can tell of such ministrations freely given by him.[33]

Nor was his own family untouched by suffering. For instance, in 1865, when Palmer himself was out of town for some weeks, they were in Columbia when it was burnt by the enemy troops, and lost all they had.

> [They] spent the night of terror in the streets, lying upon or huddled around a few bundles of bedding and clothes they had rescued from the flames. Dr. Palmer, after Columbia was evacuated, returning, first took wagons into the country to secure food for the starving women and children; and then took up his ministry to the broken-hearted people of the city.[34]

The same desire to have his life used as a vessel through which the gospel balm of healing might be poured is seen in some of his writings which became widely sought after at that time. It was in the sad years for many bereaved parents, widows and orphans, following the War Between the States, that Palmer wrote his popular volume entitled, *The Broken Home or Lessons in Sorrow*, to which we have already referred. In this volume he chose to discuss some of his own family losses in order 'to publish these and make their sorrow a means of blessing to others.'[35] He goes on to say:

> From the simple desire of comforting those who mourn, this story of repeated bereavements is here told . . . Long treasured memories are

now scattered upon the winds, with the prayer that they may help to bind up the broken-hearted.[36]

Palmer's profound compassion for the suffering was undoubtedly deepened over the years, not only by his own experience of losing his baby son in his early ministry in Columbia, but also through the deaths of four grown daughters in his later ministry in New Orleans. The daughters, including one who left a young husband and small baby, were all victims of what was then called 'consumption' – apparently the same as tuberculosis. Dr Palmer later wrote that he learned much theology as he and his wife accompanied their daughters to the very edges of the cold waters of death:

It teaches me whole volumes of theology – these tender, timid girls treading upon the fears of death and the solemnities of the tomb as if they were roses strewn upon their bridal path. I never knew before how strong grace is, nor how easy it is to walk upon the sea. My dead children have been my teachers, and I bow with awe before them.[37]

The sensitive, caring way he dealt with his own suffering children as to their spiritual conditions is indicative of his power as a soul winner, and shows how he put first things first as a father and a pastor. One example must suffice as to his gentle tact which was combined with great directness in leading people to salvation. In 1875, his daughter Gussie (whose marriage we have already seen he had so graciously encouraged) was in a dying condition with some form of consumption, some weeks after giving birth to a child. Her father had been away on ecclesiastical business for a while, and was shocked to see how much her condition had worsened during his absence. The doctor told him frankly that the end could not be far off. He was in a dilemma, for to speak to her about preparation for death too soon could so shock her that she might lose hope, but to postpone it too long could be a mistake for which he would always be sorry. The burdened father writes:

On this morning I determined to know the worst from her physician . . . I mentioned frankly [to his daughter, Gussie] what he had just said to me; but went on to speak hopefully of what might take place in her favor even yet . . . [She replied], 'I am so thankful that I was not left to put off the great matter of my salvation till this time of sickness and weakness. That is a thing already done, and somehow I have not a cloud or shadow of doubt as to my interest in Christ.'

'It is a great thing to be grateful for,' I answered, 'that God should put a check upon Satan, and not allow him to tempt you with any doubts or fears.' 'I know,' she rejoined, 'that I am a forgiven sinner; but I feel that I am forgiven and accepted.'

'Yes, my daughter, and we know that the blood of Christ cleanseth from all sin; and this blood has been already shed; we have only to rely on it and escape from the curse.'[38]

(Palmer adds that his daughter died soon afterwards in peace and victory.)

When we take together Palmer's early experience with the loss of his infant son and the much later loss of this grown daughter (as well as three others), we learn something important about his understanding of personal evangelism. His strong reliance upon the Covenant of Grace as a covenant which includes the seed of believers in the blessing of the promises of God, as well as adult believers themselves, did not make him assume that his children were automatically saved. Rather, as his frequent letters to them demonstrate, he regularly (yet kindly and tactfully) pressed the need of conversion upon them. When he wrote to them as children away from him on summer vacations, or in some cases as he sat by their very death beds, with great tenderness and conviction, he reminded them of the necessity of definite and personal repentance of sins and faith in the Lord Jesus Christ as Savior. Rather than believing that the covenant made personal soul-winning unnecessary, he felt that on the contrary, it encouraged it and caused it to bear fruit.

With this soul-winning spirit, a compassionate heart, immense pastoral diligence and anointed pulpit eloquence, it is no wonder that Dr Palmer exercised far-reaching sway for the gospel of Christ in the New Orleans area for over fifty years. And it is no wonder that such a servant of God was given many calls to distinguished posts elsewhere during his long ministry. He was offered important pulpits, a university presidency, and chairs in various seminaries, but he always turned them down so that he could remain with his people in New Orleans. In a letter to the Rev. Jos. B. Stratton in Natchez, Mississippi, in 1893, Palmer congratulates him for having spent fifty years in the Natchez church. His comments to his fellow laborer surely indicate something of his own feelings about remaining in one pulpit for most of a ministerial lifetime:

> During a pastorate of fifty years, you have touched four distinct generations: the generation which was disappearing when you first came upon the stage, the generation to which you properly belong, followed soon by that of your children, and now the hand of patriarchal blessing rests upon the heads of the children's children. What a joy to be embalmed in the grateful memories of such a constituency! And when, 'in the sweet by-and-by' you shall sit down with them all upon the mount of God, rehearsing the story of each separate life, and blending them in the universal chant of praise to Him who 'stands in the midst of the throne as a Lamb that has been slain,' then only will you know into how many blessed experiences your ministry has poured the molding influence, and there only will you know how many will claim you as one of whom 'in Christ Jesus they have been begotten through the Gospel.' Even on earth, after these generations have passed with you beyond the stars, your name will go down into the history of the church.[39]

Like his old friend in Natchez, Dr Palmer lived long enough to have the pleasure of seeing a great display of the very high regard in which he was so widely held. In 1898 on Tuesday, January 25, it seemed that the whole city of New Orleans paused to celebrate the eightieth birthday of the one who by then was generally called 'their first citizen.' A reception was held at his home from four until ten p.m., during which time some ten thousand people called on him:

> Every car coming up town carried passengers for Dr. Palmer's house . . . Amongst these were many conspicuous for their position, ecclesiastical, business, social or political. Amongst them were delegations from many benevolent, historic, religious, or patriotic institutions. Representatives of the Confederate Veterans of the division of Louisiana; Veterans of the Army of Tennessee; and Veterans of the Army of Northern Virginia in large number came with kind, loving and appreciative messages to which he responded in a manner to deepen the impression his great personality had already made upon them; saying, for example to men of the Army of Northern Virginia, that the life spent in the army was not lost, that it would bear fruit in three or four generations; that they had fought for precious principles that would not only live but be recognized as the true principles of this government.

There were representatives from three Jewish synagogues . . . Rabbi I. L. Leucht and the other officers of Touro Congregation brought with them a splendid solid silver loving cup inscribed with Dr. Palmer's initials, in the form of a handsome monogram; with the legend, 'Presented to Rev. B. M. Palmer, D.D., by the Rabbi and Board of Officers of Touro Synagogue on the day of his reaching fourscore years, January 25, 1898,' and with the following selection from Psalm 89 verse 28: 'For evermore will I keep for him my kindness; and my covenant shall stand fast with him.'[40]

He received telegrams and letters from Roman Catholic Cardinal Gibbons, from the Episcopal Bishop of Louisiana, Dr Sessums, from Princeton and Southwestern Universities, and from scholars, pastors, churches and newspapers up and down the entire East Coast. However, probably no letter touched him as deeply as the one from the infirm inhabitants of the Old Soldiers' Home in Louisiana:

Reverend sir, there are now near seven score of us in this refuge, this camp, bronzed and tattered veterans. Our strength and usefulness have departed. We are all more or less afflicted by disease, by the weaknesses incidental to old age. Some are maimed, have lost limbs . . . We have outlived everything but the memory of the great conflict, and we owe our present support and comfort to the benevolence of the State of Louisiana, for which we fought . . .

Your name, your memory, and, above all, your continued presence with us, invoke our gratitude to the everlasting Father for sparing you to us, for we recognize in you a living link with the past. In common with all the surviving soldiers of our beloved Southland, we love and esteem our battle pastor. We remember our debt to you, your fortitude and constancy in the dark hours, your striking example engendering in us those moral qualities . . .[41]

He was also honored in 1898 by having an orphanage named for him by its founders: the session of the Presbyterian Church of Columbus, Mississippi. This strong Christian institution still continues to serve needy children nearly a century later. The story of its founding and its being named for B. M. Palmer is told by the late Rev. C. W. Grafton of Union Church, Mississippi.[42]

Dr Palmer lived for four more years, and remained true to his original trust: preaching, visiting and praying until he was hit by a street car in the May of 1902. This accident proved fatal, although he lingered for several days. He died in great peace and was mourned all across the land as newspapers carried the story of how the great preacher had laid down the silver trumpet of redemption below to take his place in the white-robed choirs above. As he himself said at the funeral of his beloved elder, Joseph A. Maybin, some years earlier, 'in the shadow of the night, the Lord Himself came down and took him in His arms and bore him upward to his crown and to His throne.'[43]

10

THE CHARACTERISTICS OF PALMER'S MINISTRY

Palmer's writings and statesmanship in church and state, fruitful as they were, cannot compare in depth, breadth and perpetuity of influence with his gospel preaching. I first became aware of the beauties of Palmer's preaching when, serving a student internship in a church in rural North Carolina, I discovered two volumes of his sermons in the church library. From time to time I enjoyed and greatly benefited from dipping into these volumes. I shall never forget how I was particularly impressed, those twenty years ago, with two sermons he preached on 'The Death of Believers No Evidence Against Their Justification.' His biographer, Thomas Cary Johnson (also the biographer and successor of Robert L. Dabney) describes Palmer's preaching in these terms:

> He was a real preacher of the Gospel. He had studied the evidences of its being the word of God; had deliberately made up his mind that they were valid, and that the Bible is the word of God; had set that down as a fixed fact in his creed. He gave himself to preaching that word. Whatever others might preach, science, sociology, politics, literature, he would preach the Gospel, and the Gospel only, from his pulpit. It was a thing the world needed worst of all, and that need he would fill. He preached the Westminster interpretation of the Bible, preached it all; the doctrines of the Trinity and the incarnation; the doctrines of sin and grace, the doctrine of the atonement, the doctrines of regeneration and conversion, justification and sanctification. He even preached boldly and frequently on those points of Calvinism which have been so bitterly attacked in every generation, viz.: total depravity, unconditional election,

particular redemption, efficacious grace and perseverance therein unto the end.

He was a theological preacher from the very order of his mind. He was bound to systematize, to theorize facts, to endeavour to discover their philosophy . . . Knowing the truth of the Bible experimentally, and preaching what by experience he knew to be true, he communicated, as by a contagion, the affection of his own mind to the truth. To the minds thus opened he poured in the great central doctrines of Christianity. He was particularly happy in preaching the great doctrine of the atonement by the cross, but the gift of popularization of all the great doctrines was his. He was a living refutation of the widely current notion that the day of doctrinal preaching is over.[44]

Palmer preached far more frequently and for a longer period of time than any of the other men we discuss in this volume. In addition, for about two years, his sermons were printed weekly, thus providing us with a wealth of material that we simply do not possess from Thornwell and Girardeau. From my perspective, I would say that he combines the majesty of Thornwell's piercing logic and elegant language with the sweetness, humanity, drawing power and approachability of Girardeau. Though highly structured, he manages to avoid the overly close logical reasoning which was employed by Thornwell and to a lesser extent by Girardeau. Indeed, there is a constant element of sweetness and beauty in the preaching of Palmer which is rarely found in such rich measure, so that, in my opinion, his sermons make far better reading today than those of either of these men.

This unusual grace and beauty of proclamation seemed to lend a certain attractiveness to Palmer's otherwise unimpressive physical appearance. During a commencement address on 'The Present Crisis and its Issue' at Washington and Lee University, some distinguished observers made these remarkable comments about Palmer's preaching and appearance:

It is of this occasion that Dr. S. H. Chester writes the story of the Honorable John Randolph Tucker and Commodore M. F. Maury. They were seated on the rostrum. Commodore Maury said to Mr. Tucker, as Dr. Palmer began speaking: 'He is the ugliest man I ever saw.' Ten minutes later he said: 'He is getting better looking.' Near the close of the magnificent address, he turned again to Mr. Tucker and said: 'He is the handsomest man I ever saw, sir.'[45]

* * *

We must go on to consider several specific characteristics of Palmer's preaching which gave it such beauty and healing power to appreciative multitudes.

In the first place, we must note how Palmer drew his sermons from the biblical text. In the words of T. C. Johnson:

> Capable of the finest expository preaching, he was driven by the bent of his mind to topical preaching very largely. In this method the logical and systematizing tendencies have the freest and noblest application. His plan, usually, then, upon announcing his text, was to show exactly what the text, in its historical setting connections, meant. This he did by a careful exegesis, giving often, in this preliminary step, as much matter, and in better form, as many ministers put into a whole sermon. Then having set forth in perspicuous terms the doctrinal teaching, which he had drawn from the text, he would proceed to enforce it by a series of arguments, generally powerful in themselves and so happily put as to carry general conviction . . . Following this would come an application which was often threefold, or more, in the course of which the truth, previously developed by interpretation and argument, would be pressed with all his powers of appeal and persuasion.[46]

Palmer, then, was not an exegetical, expository preacher in the manner of some of the best preachers of our own generation. Yet he listened carefully to the biblical text, though in a more systematic-theological sense than in a thoroughly historico-grammatical-literary sense. Using R. B. Kuiper's terminology, Dr Morton Smith has suggested that Palmer's preaching is 'analytic-synthetic.'[47] By 'analytic', Kuiper meant essentially a kind of running commentary on the biblical text, interspersed with application such as was found in the preaching of the great John Chrysostom and many sixteenth-century Protestant Reformers. By 'synthetic', he meant 'thematic preaching' with more logically organized discussion of a theme, though with less exegetical detail. I tend to think that Dr Smith is right in holding that Palmer combines the two, although I would certainly think that Palmer leans very heavily in the synthetic direction – too much so at times.

* * *

A second feature of his preaching is that it was and is able to hold the hearer's (reader's) interest.

Dr John Reed Miller, who was for many years the distinguished pastor of First Presbyterian Church of Jackson, Mississippi, often says, 'It is not a sin to be interesting in our preaching!' It is obvious that to have held the attention of 1,500 people each Sunday for several decades, Palmer was of necessity a most interesting preacher. As a general rule, most of us find the reading of old sermons to be a rather boring exercise. Yet, I repeat my testimony that it is a delightful and uplifting experience to read the sermons of Palmer today, even a century after they were originally preached. In this sense Palmer is like Spurgeon: they are both members of that very select company whose sermons are well worth reading long after they were first heard.

It is not easy to state precisely why Palmer's sermons, or indeed those of anyone else, are interesting, but we must try to isolate one or two important factors. First, he always had a clear outline so that the congregation could easily understand what he meant to say and how each new point related to the message as a whole. This type of approach, in the words of R. B. Kuiper, 'makes for unity . . . it offers a better opportunity for the comparison of Scripture with Scripture and so lends itself admirably to the setting forth of the system of truth taught in the Bible.'[48] In Palmer's hands, this skill gives a definite beauty to his preaching in that it enables the hearer to perceive an attractively ordered movement of thought from introduction to conclusion. For my own part, the beauty of the creatively ordered structure of his sermons makes me think of the landscape paintings of someone like Constable.

Let us take two or three illustrations of Palmer's carefully crafted outlines. We mentioned earlier his two remarkable sermons on the subject, 'The Death of Believers No Evidence Against Their Justification.' These two sermons were delivered on successive Sabbaths according to his not infrequent practice of giving two sermons on one text, so that he could explore and apply it more fully. The text upon which these sermons is based is Romans 8:10–11: 'And if Christ be in you, the body is dead because of sin; but the Spirit is life because of righteousness. But if the Spirit of him that raised up Jesus from the dead dwell in you, he that raised up Christ from the dead shall also quicken your mortal bodies by his Spirit that dwelleth in you.'

After skillfully placing these verses in their broader and narrower context, Palmer then outlines his two messages as follows:

I. The body is the instrument with which we sin, and through which that sin is made patent to the observation of others.
II. It is not the design of grace to take evil out of the world, as to its being; but only to destroy its penal character, and to convert it into an instrument of spiritual discipline.
III. The body of the Christian must die in order to its sanctification, that it may be fitted for the world of glory.
IV. The sudden translation of believers without death, would subvert the principle of grace, which is the ground principle of the whole Gospel scheme.
V. The successive translation of believers, without dying, would anticipate the decisions of the judgment day, and rob the resurrection morn of its glory.

In his second sermon, after a brief recapitulation, he states that he does not wish to discuss the whole doctrine of the resurrection, 'but only to enlarge the two grounds upon which it is based in the text, to-wit: *the connexion between the believer and Christ, and the indwelling of the Holy Ghost*.'[49] His outline is:

I. The body of the saint will be raised because equally redeemed by Christ and equally, with the soul, united to Him.
II. The body of the saint will be raised because of the indwelling of the Holy Ghost.

He then concludes with 'two important references':

(1) These moral grounds of the resurrection satisfy us as to its certainty, and bear us over all the difficulties with which it is invested.
(2) The comfort is precious which flows from this truth, in view of death both to ourselves and to those whom we love.

By contrast, the structure of the two sermons on John 17:24 ('Christ's Prayer for His People') is rather more closely tied to the specific text than the two sermons we have just considered. He outlined the first sermon in the following way:

I. [This prayer of Christ] expresses the perfect confidence which Christ has in the reality and extent of His Father's love.

II. We detect here the oneness of Christ's will with that of the Father.
III. This language is justified upon the ground of the covenant and grant, which the Father has made to the Son as Mediator.
IV. This language, thus imperative, recognizes Christ's claim as founded upon His own purchase by blood.
V. This language is uttered by Christ as the Head of His seed; and this constitutes it a testamentary word.
VI. This peculiar language is the language of royalty.
VII. This language of Christ, 'I WILL,' indicates that the whole glory of God is a pledge that this promise shall be redeemed.

Again, after a brief recapitulation, the second sermon opens with the statement that having discussed the *manner* of this prayer, now he will discuss its *matter*. Thus:

I. We are presented with Christ's personal longing to have His children with Him in heaven.
- (1) This springs from His infinite goodness, and the love which, as our Redeemer, He bears to His people.
- (2) This language expresses, again, the longing of Christ's human soul for human fellowship.
- (3) Christ desires the presence of His redeemed in heaven, as the representatives of His passion and death.
- (4) The redeemed are desired by Jesus in heaven because they constitute His portion and reward.

II. . . .The plea is filed . . . (that) they are to be with Him, where He is, that they may behold His glory.
- (1) We shall behold our Lord in His glorified humanity.
- (2) Another element of this glory will be the perfect righteousness through which He has 'magnified the law and made it honorable.'
- (3) The third element in this glory of Christ will be the glory of His universal Headship.
- (4) There is the glory of Jesus, as all the mediatorial offices are united in Him.
- (5) We shall behold the glory of Christ in His oneness with the Father.

Along with the comprehensibility which flowed from his clear outlines was the obvious care he took not to overload his messages with too much material. He knew that it was all too easy for a congregation to be choked with so many facts that they lose the main point of the text. Thus he avoided a significant characteristic of the preaching of the great Dabney. Their biographer, Thomas C. Johnson, has stated that Dabney packed so much material into one sermon that other preachers could find enough to keep them supplied for six sermons! While such an approach can be beneficial when handled by a highly skilled 'master of assemblies' like Dr Dabney, if most preachers were to use it they would run the risk of confusing and discouraging their congregations, and cause them to rapidly lose their concentration. In Dr Dabney's case, however, this does not seem to have happened. He was evidently one of those rare individuals who can give much content *and* hold people's attention. But Palmer, for all his abilities, was wise in understanding that to maintain people's interest, he had to measure out the truth in digestible portions.

Another important factor which lends such compelling interest to the preaching of Palmer was his ability to concentrate attention on the point at hand by using human illustrations which touch real life, rather like the parables of Christ or the visions of Amos, or the enacted parables of Jeremiah. For example, in a sermon on 'The Antidote of Care,' he presents several brief, poignant illustrations on the overcoming of discontentment. Then he says: 'These illustrations, you will admit, are tableaux of real life . . .'[50] Many are the passages where Palmer speaks of deathbed scenes (though always preserving a chaste respect and avoiding any lurid sentimentalism), of businesses in bankruptcy (or prospering), of wayward children (or of happy parents), etc.

Elsewhere, he uses, for example, illustrations of a magnet, a bird in a cage, and a man in the Sahara Desert;[51] he explains the impartation of Christian character in terms of a photograph;[52] he vividly describes the organs of the body as the medium of worship.[53] Perhaps surprisingly for a conservative Calvinist in the nineteenth century, he actually introduced one sermon by telling the story of a character in a contemporary English novel.[54] (We remember that Dabney had written an article against the reading of novels!) In other words, he does not live on some exalted mountain top, but is down where people live, a quality which is so necessary if our preaching is to be interesting. It is surely this evidence of contact with daily life that lends such continuing attraction and attention to his sermons.

* * *

A third feature of Palmer's ministry was profound sympathy allied to a realistic pastoral insight.

We mentioned earlier how he spoke of his desire to put a drop of balm into the wounds of the suffering, and undoubtedly the most distinctive attribute of Palmer's preaching is its encouraging nature. Indeed, the very word he uses to describe his own conversion is 'balm'. Speaking of the peace which Christ brings, he said, 'through five and fifty years it has deepened in the soul to which it came as the balm of heaven.' The balm of Gilead had surely touched his own soul and thus he knew of the value it could have for others. One thinks of Palmer, especially in those post-war years, as administering grace and restoration to an entire generation through his preaching ministrations.

Now we must ask, precisely how did he pour out this balm on the suffering through his preaching? One of the major truths through which the gospel balm was imparted to his hearers was the love of God in his providence. So many of his sermons express the sense of Cowper's hymn stanzas:

> Ye fearful saints, fresh courage take;
> The clouds ye so much dread
> Are big with mercy, and shall break
> In blessings on your head.
>
> Judge not the Lord by feeble sense,
> But trust Him for His grace;
> Behind a frowning providence
> He hides a smiling face.

In a sermon preached in 1857 he spoke of the darkness of providence and of God's good plan for us. In a moving passage – relevant for any century – he encourages parents to keep on praying for their lost children.[55] In another, 'Victory Over Trials,' he lifts us up by reminding us that trials will not be allowed to break us:

> . . . Let us make the most of our trials. They may be severe; but in this severity, they may be the particular form in which it pleases our Father that we shall give our testimony. In that case our sorrow is our glory. There is many a bed-ridden saint, who for years has been tossing upon the couch of weariness and of pain, and experiencing a

thousand martyrdoms. He is a witness for the grace of God. He is, as truly as Daniel in the lions' den, a prophet for God . . . Oh! it is a crown, brother, for you, not of shame nor of dishonor, if, in the patient endurance of affliction and reproach, you are able to turn to God and feel that he will at last make you *more than conqueror* through Him that loved you. Do not be afraid, in the utmost severity of God's discipline, that He will pass the bounds of a just measure.

The human heart is like a harp, and all these affections are but the chords of that harp; and the only being who knows skillfully to play upon that harp, is He that made it. If He, the Master of the song, turns the screw, and strains the chord even until it threatens to snap, do not fear. 'The man of sorrows and acquainted with grief,' who went down into the bowels of the curse for redemption – He is the musician whose hands are upon the chords and keys of this mysterious instrument. He will turn those screws, and stretch those chords to the point when they should crack and part. But no, He only brings them to the right tension; so that when His blessed finger shall sweep across the strings, each shall give its proper note – and all shall blend in eternal harmony of praise unto '*Him that loves us*'[56]

He has some remarkable passages on the believer's joy in dying,[57] on personal individuality in heaven,[58] and a golden paragraph on the value of faithfully serving God into old age:

It is not worth our while to live longer than three score years and ten if those years have, each of them, been made a stepping-stone by which we have risen higher in wisdom and higher in grace, and are prepared for the contemplation of the great God. There is no occasion of regret, my friend, if the gray hair hangs over your brow, and admonishes that the next step will be across the border, and will plant you within the circuit of that kingdom where all these glories will be developed to your view. Consider, too, that the knowledge which man gains on earth is acquired with infinite labor; whereas, in the world above, all will come just as easily as seeing . . .

Take a boy of six, poring over his multiplication table, and with almost incredible difficulty mastering the first elements of figures; and then take the man of sixty, who has ascended above the multiplication table to the comprehension of all science, is able to put his foot upon those distant stars, and walks with the imperial march of a monarch along the milky way with which God belts the sky as though it were the highway to His own palace, and see the immense stride which has been made from six to sixty.

Apply this measure to the eternal world – when we have been fifty years in heaven, have gazed for fifty years upon all the glories of

Jehovah . . . until the accumulation of centuries swells beyond your powers of computation . . . what shall be the largeness of the human intellect there? How great shall the man be who has been but a short eternity in heaven? Can any of you tell how Moses and Paul, and all those who in God's Book have disclosed His will, have grown during the short period they in eternity have been gazing upon the splendors of Jehovah's throne? Brethren, it makes a man pant to be there. One longs to make a spring over the gulf that separates the two worlds.[59]

He also speaks with profound insight and tender care of denied prayers, and how in 'the infinite wisdom of our Father in heaven, the prayer is answered in the very denial of the *special petition*.'[60] He holds out glorious hope for a sinful church,[61] and for a sinful world.[62]

Surely the reason for Palmer's ability to be so encouraging as he rubbed the gospel balm into the wounds of his people is to be found in the following combination of qualities which underlay the work of the great preacher. No-one can deal with people in an effective pastoral manner until he understands their circumstances. He knew exactly where his people stood, and therefore had the right combination of medicine for them. Dr John Miller Wells has written, 'He was at his best in comforting those in sorrow. He was gifted in ministering to the brokenhearted.'[63] Small and great looked to him for help. For instance, the widow of the late President of the Confederacy, Jefferson Davis, once wrote:

About a year before my husband died he became very restless and announced his intention to go to New Orleans. We had several guests in the house and I suggested his waiting until Monday, but he said decidedly, 'I want to go today'. It was Saturday. He came back on Monday evening very calm and cheerful. In a day or two he said, 'I went to commune with Dr. Palmer, and it has done me a world of good . . .' Something had disquieted him greatly and he went to Dr. Palmer for comfort.[64]

In his preaching, Palmer was able to communicate to the people his profound understanding of their feelings, fears, anxieties and griefs. This he could do without either threatening them with ministerial displeasure or superiority on the one hand, or sentimentally accepting, without challenge, destructive attitudes on the other hand. That is, he could expose hurtful feelings in a non-condemnatory way, while simultaneously opening a door of hope which seemed realistically very close by. In one sermon he speaks of the feelings of the many widows in his congregation with 'crepe veils over their faces'.[65] He does the same with many other categories of needy persons.

One passage of Palmer makes us think of the remarkable pastoral counseling that the late Martyn Lloyd-Jones was able to accomplish in his preaching. Indeed the passage has the ring of the twentieth century's straightforwardness to it:

> Should any of you come to me for counsel under the burden of your anxieties, I would probably address you in terms like the following: Are not these cares incident to the relations you sustain in life, and did not God bind them up together? Did you not yourselves select these relations, with the foreknowledge of their attendant cares? Would you even now consent to drop those, in order to be quiet of these? If a parent, would you be willing to be deprived of your children to be rid of their trouble?[66]

* * *

In the fourth place we may say that Palmer's life and preaching was characterized by total commitment to the Word of God and by reliance upon the sufferings, death and resurrection of Jesus Christ.

John Owen is alleged to have said that sermons must be like root vegetables, and boiled in the corner of the fireplace for a long time before they are ready to be served! Palmer evidently identified with this sentiment, and thought for months or years on certain passages upon which he wished to preach. For example, he even wrote that he had contemplated for years the words of Christ, 'My peace I leave with you,' in the hope of preaching a series of sermons on it but still he was unable to do so.[67]

Besides the hard work of long thinking, Palmer carefully and painfully interacted with the biblical text in the original language (at least that is the case with the Greek), not forgetting to pay attention to the historical and grammatical context of each passage. He specifically dealt with Greek grammar in various places,[68] and mentions the importance of proper exegesis.[69] He is also very competent at dealing with both the larger and smaller context.[70]

While Palmer held strongly to the necessity of the illumination of the Holy Spirit within the believer for the apprehension of spiritual truth, he refused to allow the possibility of new revelations and spiritual pretensions which could undercut the written Word. Speaking of 'The Sealing of the Spirit,' he says:

> He simply takes the things which belong to Jesus Christ and shows them unto us. The sphere of His illumination is the written Word; and this is our protection against fanaticism. Said Luther, when the mystics of his day raved around him of their secret inspiration, in the impatience and scorn which belonged to his strong heart, 'I slap your spirit upon its snout.' All revelations must be brought to the law and to the testimony . . . Avaunt, avaunt, as specters from the world of darkness, all these revelations of spirits! God has spoken in the person of His own Son. Who shall come after Jesus Christ? . . . shall we have, after this, the babblings of spirits conjured up around a table in a darkened room? We need no other revelations, since we have the utterance of God's own thoughts, through the speech of His own Son and by the inspiration of the Holy Ghost.[71]

Finally we must note that with the keen insight of a wise winner of souls, Palmer cuts away every other possible crutch or assistance from the way of salvation, and leaves the sinful soul face to face with the Lord Jesus Christ. One day, a young man who was dying in the epidemic of 1867 said in great fear to Dr Palmer, 'I shall soon be in eternity, and I am not ready.' Then he asked, 'Is there any meeting going on in any of the churches, that I may have a chance to get religion?' Palmer, with great wisdom, replied:

> Ah, you must not rely upon anything of that sort now. Your salvation lies between your own soul and God, and you have no need of any meeting in this or that church. Here is the Savior, who comes to you with the promise, 'Him that cometh unto me I will in no wise cast out'. Gather up your thoughts in the few moments that are left you, and cast your soul upon that Redeemer. Cry out to Him, as Peter did when sinking in the waters, 'Lord, save or I perish'; and feel that nothing can deliver you from these terrible apprehensions, but the cross of Jesus Christ.[72]

In the good mercy of God, that young man did cry out to God and by and by found peace of soul. Surely, we have no less need today to be on guard lest something, even (and indeed, especially) something ecclesiastical, come between seeking souls and the salvation personally offered by the crucified, glorified Redeemer of God's elect. For instance, several years ago at a social occasion, a young lady from another denomination asked the summer assistant minister at a Presbyterian church in South Carolina, how could anyone possibly be saved in a church which did not issue a regular invitation to walk down the aisle at the close of the service! Without a moment's hesitation, and with some force, the young assistant answered: 'By God!'

The fact that our salvation comes directly and entirely and sovereignly from God alone is the key that opens our understanding to the wonderful power and effects of the preaching of Girardeau, Thornwell, Baker and Palmer. What was the source of their effectiveness? They all came from the same place, from the glorified Jesus, our great High Priest, seated on the throne of his mediatorial power. And if we today are to have something of their qualities, we too must seek it from the same place in the same way. Let us go on our faces before the Lamb of God and cry out to him for these blessings so that 'He may see of the travail of his soul and be satisfied' (Isa. 53:11).

PART FOUR

JOHN L. GIRARDEAU: UNCTION AT WORK

11

'SOUTH CAROLINA IS MY MOTHER'

Both Old and New Testaments make clear that one of the major characteristics of the Messiah and of the Messianic Age is that the Spirit of the Lord would so anoint him (and his emissaries) that the gospel would be preached to the poor and the brokenhearted would be healed (cf. Isa. 61 and Luke 4). The Gospels show us that the poor heard him gladly, and the remarkable, loving, compassionate and receptive relationship between Jesus and the poor has continued to be true of those who know Jesus best and the needy classes of their own generation. Thus the outstanding characteristic and greatest legacy of the life and preaching of John L. Girardeau lies precisely here: first in his love and self-consecration to the neglected sea-coast blacks of antebellum South Carolina, then in their glad responsiveness to his ministrations, and finally in the unusual way the Holy Spirit honored the personal and preaching relationship between this white, Southern minister and black slave (and then freedman).

Before we can appreciate the unique preaching ministry of Girardeau, we must first look in some detail at his life. As his name indicates, Girardeau was of French Huguenot descent. He was born in 1825 to a Presbyterian family on James Island, S.C., not far from Charleston. Though raised on a fairly remote cotton plantation, there was a church not too far away where the doctrines of grace were preached whenever services were held. His family was faithful in attendance, and in his early years he saw his parents and other relatives involved in a series of fervent prayer meetings which seem to have been blessed with a visitation of the Spirit of God.

He lost his mother at the age of seven, and though he felt it keenly, he later wrote: 'I think I can distinctly see how it has worked for ultimate good ... We lost the benefit of her motherly care and instruction, but we gained the benefit of tuition in the school of affliction; and eternity alone will reveal how important that discipline was.'[1] Thus, at this early age, young Girardeau was already experiencing, and would continue to experience throughout his life, that inner brokenness and personal loss which so paradoxically issues forth in streams of resurrection influence from the life of the broken one to others: 'So then, death worketh in us, but life in you' (2 Cor. 4:12). We cannot doubt that the loss of his mother as well as his childhood rural loneliness were factors in that unseen inner chemistry that would later give him such an open, compassionate heart for the slaves of his region.

At the age of ten he was sent to school in Charleston, where he remained until the end of his college career. In addition to his successfully mastering Greek, Latin, French, mathematics and all the other elementary subjects, something far more wonderful happened: the grace of Christ came down and mastered young student Girardeau. Just before he turned fifteen, Girardeau finished high school and entered the College of Charleston. He had regularly attended Second Presbyterian Church under the preaching of the faithful and eloquent Calvinist preacher, Dr Thomas Smyth, but was still unconverted. As he entered college, he underwent a month of terrible conviction and utter gloom:

> He was afraid to put out his light at night lest the darkness should never end. He was afraid to go to sleep lest he should awake in the company of the damned. He had no appetite for food. He could not study. No earthly thing interested him. He spent his time reading the Bible, calling on God for mercy and bemoaning his lost estate. In vain did he strive to make peace with God; he wept over the consequences of his sins, but there was no sense of pardon; he tried to repent and reform, but there was no peace; he strove to make covenants and agreements with God, but the earth was iron and the heavens were brass.[2]

Yet during this hard time he undertook some very serious reading for a fifteen-year-old. In Girardeau's own handwriting, at the end of his copy of the *Memoirs of Thomas Halyburton*, he noted in later years some of his favorite authors as well as the particular book he was reading just before his conversion:

Over and over again have I read this remarkable dying experience. Lord, help me in my last hour! Calvin, Owen, Witsius, Halyburton and Thornwell have been among the chief of my instructors. The account of Wilberforce Richmond's dying experience in Grimshaw's 'Legh Richmond's Domestic Portraiture,' was the proximate instrument in the hands of the ever blessed Spirit of leading me to believe in Jesus. It was at the north corner of King Street and Price's Alley in Charleston. Oh, the unutterable rapture of that hour when I found him, after a month's conflict with sin and hell! The heavens and the earth seemed to be singing psalms of praise for redeeming love.[3]

Elsewhere, George A. Blackburn, his biographer, explains more fully what transpired in this great transaction which neither Girardeau nor his Savior would ever retract:

One beautiful morning while on his knees begging for mercy, it occurred to him that he had already done everything that it was possible for him to do, and that all of these things had availed him nothing. He would, therefore, just surrender himself to Jesus and leave the case in his hands. This was faith. Instantly the Holy Spirit assured him that he was accepted in Christ, that his sins were forgiven, and that God loved him with an everlasting love.

He sprang to his feet, clapped his hands and poured out the overflowing joy of his soul in praise. All nature had changed. In the description of his feelings he said that the sun shone brighter, the birds sang sweeter, and the breezes blew softer than he had ever known them to do. His flesh as well as his heart felt the delight of the presence of a reconciled God. He could see no reason why any intelligent creature could care to do anything in this world but love and praise God.[4]

Elsewhere, George A. Blackburn, who was also the son-in-law of Girardeau, in a powerful understatement, says of this conversion: 'This experience left its stamp on his whole life. The trace of that month, with its horrors and its joys, can be seen in his thinking, his preaching and his living.'[5] It does seem clear from church history that a profound knowledge of having passed from death to life is an essential part of the equipment of the truly evangelical preacher. Having faced the horrors of hell and foretasted the joys of heaven in his own soul, Girardeau would always maintain the firmest grasp on the reality and all-surpassing importance of God and the unseen spiritual world. It is evident that Girardeau keenly felt the truth which he preached; his congregations could sense that he felt it, and they in turn found it hard to remain indifferent to what so gripped his powerful mind and character.

After college, Girardeau served as tutor for a year in the home of a planter some eight miles from Charleston, and soon thereafter became engaged to the planter's daughter, Penelope Sarah Hamlin. From 1845–48 he attended Columbia Theological Seminary, which was then, of course, still in Columbia, S.C. Probably no two men were more influential on his thinking and future preaching than his seminary professors. These were none other than James H. Thornwell, whom Girardeau often heard in chapel, and who was then President of South Carolina College, and B. M. Palmer, who, as we have also seen, was the current, popular preacher of the First Presbyterian Church of Columbia. During his time at Columbia Seminary, his compassion for the poor and socially disadvantaged manifested itself in mission services that he conducted in an abandoned warehouse in the destitute section of town. Owing to these regular evangelistic efforts, many broken and abandoned persons – including several prostitutes – professed saving faith in Jesus Christ. Girardeau's tender spirit towards those who were sinful, needy and hurting, reminds one somewhat of Francis A. Schaeffer's outreach to drunken students when he was at Hampden-Sydney College in Virginia in the 1930s.

After graduation in 1848, Girardeau was licensed by the presbytery of Charleston as pulpit supply for various rural churches in the Charleston area. Even in these relatively backwoods areas with scanty populations, his preaching and pastoral care constantly attracted overflow crowds of both blacks and whites. Some even walked as far as twenty miles to hear the young, powerful preacher, who had such obvious zeal for their salvation. Then in 1849, he married his fiancée, who, though she came from a wealthy plantation society background, gladly relinquished its luxuries in order to consecrate herself along with her husband to the only important thing that would matter in eternity: the glorifying of God through serving, loving and winning precious souls to Christ and teaching them to observe all things commanded in the Holy Word. Their long marriage seems to have been one of mutual benefit and Christian joy, and they were blessed with ten children. Several sons became elders in the Presbyterian Church, and several of their daughters married Presbyterian ministers and theologians, including George A. Blackburn, father of the well-known John C. Blackburn, and Robert A. Webb, theological author and professor at Louisville Seminary.

Before we outline the rest of Girardeau's eventful life, it seems essential to pinpoint some of his controlling spiritual, personal characteristics. These are often difficult to define, but are the all-important fountain of motives and source of energy, or, to change the figure, they form the moral, spiritual and intellectual grid through which the world is interpreted and met. We must attempt a glimpse at this inner precinct of the soul in order to understand the rather unconventional choices he would make and the unexpected directions he would take throughout the remainder of his pilgrimage.

The psalmist says, 'All my springs are in thee' (Ps. 87:7), and in the truest sense, the deep places of Girardeau's life were continually filled with that vital, resurrection existence that belongs to all who 'abide in Christ'. Indeed, as we shall see, one of the perennial themes of his preaching and later of his theological teaching and writing was the doctrine so central in St Paul's theology and so architectonic in John Calvin's interpretation of the Christian life: union with Christ. This experiental, transforming union of the believer with his incarnate, crucified, risen and glorified Savior and Lord, was viewed by Girardeau in the broader context of a robust Trinitarian theology as mediated through two lines. First there was the Augustinian and Calvinist grasp of grace and second the Westminster, Puritan exposition of the covenants with their emphasis on the federal headship of Adam and Christ.

While we may properly think of Girardeau as a sincere adherent and learned exponent of the finest theology of British Puritanism, it is necessary to remember that he had much in common with most other Presbyterian Christians in the pre-1930 Southeastern Atlantic seaboard. For them all, the incomparable intellectual precision of the Westminster doctrines were filtered through the uniquely Southern experience of a Bible-based culture which was periodically showered with the warm fervency of revival blessing. This peculiarly Southern Presbyterian approach to theology and life could perhaps be thought of as a further development of the Covenanting Scottish piety of the 'Second Reformation' of the 1630s and 1640s. Transplanted on these shores, it was rekindled and reworked through the heat and power of the mighty Great Awakening of the 1740s and the longer Second Great Awakening which lasted from the 1780s into the 1830s. The combination of the British Puritan background of its population and the continuance of these revival movements meant that even before the 1830s, America had a 'Bible Belt'. This designation particularly fits the Southern colonies, as Dr Morton Smith points out in his fine *Studies in Southern Presbyterian Theology*.[6]

This does not mean that evangelical Christianity experienced no resistance from the Southern culture. On the contrary, the spiritual and societal power of the Second Great Awakening in particular is vividly demonstrated by contrasting it with the widespread anti-theistic influences in much of the post-revolutionary South (which stemmed from the French Enlightenment). These Deistic and even atheistic forces were largely overwhelmed and transformed by the strength of the revival. E. Brooks Holifield properly points out 'the skepticism and infidelity' of this time, but fails to note that the evangelical re-awakening which swept the South was nothing new.[7] That is perhaps one reason (from the human perspective) why the Second Great Awakening had wider and easier reception and a longer-lasting influence in the South than elsewhere. It was, in a certain sense, a peculiarly 'native' movement in the South. It was felt to be part and parcel of the traditional religious heritage of the region's British Protestant ancestors.

Thus at its very best, the traditional Southern Presbyterian mentality can be accurately described as combining two attitudes. On the one hand, there was immense respect for the highest intellectual, theological learning, manifested in the Presbyterian emphasis on higher education with a consequent channeling of significant resources to the building of schools and colleges. But secondly, there could be found personal, heart religion, manifested in an unashamed devotion to Jesus, literal acceptance of Scripture and thirsty longing for Spirit-sent revival. These combined attributes are as true of Girardeau as they were of Samuel Davies, Moses Hoge, Archibald Alexander, all of whom lived before him, and Thornwell, Palmer and Dabney among his contemporaries. Not all forms of Calvinism have been marked by this balance between intellect and heart, but that, at its best, is Southern Presbyterianism in general, and the soul of Girardeau in particular.

Closely allied to John Girardeau's love of theology was his fascination with a host of philosophical questions which are vitally intertwined with religion. Dr Thornton Whaling, who was President of Columbia Seminary after Girardeau retired, spoke of his mentor (Girardeau) as 'the philosopher of Southern Presbyterianism'.[8] In our own day, Dr John Leith of Union Seminary in Richmond has expressed regret at the twentieth-century neglect of Girardeau, who, he suggests, probably had the greatest philosophical interest of any Southern Presbyterian thinker.[9] This philosophical interest was, I would submit, part and parcel of his vital experience of the reality of God, the soul and the spiritual world. In the line of the Scottish School of Common Sense Realism (particularly as introduced to this country by John Witherspoon of Scotland and then Princeton), Girardeau followed Thornwell, Alexander and others in seeking a strong and clear refutation of the implicit atheism and skepticism of David Hume and other secularist Enlightenment thinkers. His philosophical bent, however, would not play a significant part until much later in his ministerial career. In the meantime, more specifically theological and practical concerns would predominate, such as preaching the gospel to the lost (both black and white), building up the church, and defending his beloved Confederacy against massive enemy onslaught.

In addition to the Calvinist commitments of his soul, Girardeau was, from start to finish, a cultural Southerner, and more specifically an undyingly loyal son of the state of South

Carolina. Unless we take this aspect of the 'chemistry' of his soul into consideration, we shall not understand his ministry. State loyalty and local pride is perhaps a dying thing in the mobile, rootless television culture of so much of modern America, but until fairly recently, it has powerfully shaped the personal experience and community culture of many of us, not to mention our Southern ancestors. This profound love of South Carolina which possessed him from earliest youth and so shaped his preaching career is attractively illustrated by two events that occurred in his middle and latter ministry. To jump ahead in his life's story, when he returned to South Carolina after having served in the Confederate army for some years in Virginia, he literally climbed out of the wagon and kissed the very soil!

A number of years later, after he was a professor at the seminary in Columbia, a wealthy and distinguished church in Atlanta, Georgia, issued a strong call inviting him to be its pastor. Dr Joseph Mack, a close friend of Girardeau's, who had personal ties with the calling church in Atlanta, pressed him as to why he was declining the call. With some agitation, Girardeau replied:

> I will tell you now why I cannot accept that call, though I never expected to tell anyone. By the grace of God I was born in this State, through the mercy of God my home all my life has been in this State, and it is my heart's desire and prayer that my lifeless body shall sleep beneath its sod until the resurrection morn. South Carolina is my mother. She now needs the service of her sons. I would rather accept $400.00 and a cabin in a country church of South Carolina than the $4,000.00 and the splendid manse in the magnificent city of Atlanta.[10]

A recent article by a Northern scholar who spends a considerable amount of time in North Carolina suggests that this kind of love for one's state is still a Southern characteristic. He expressed amazement at, and appreciation for, the strong and enduring pride and love that Carolinians have for their native state.[11] According to him, this sort of attitude is not the case in places such as New Jersey!

Not only was Girardeau's soul 'bound in a bundle of life' with South Carolina, the Palmetto State, he also particularly loved his native Low Country. A sermon which he preached in

Charleston after the end of the war, vividly painting scenes of the beloved Low Country life, touched deep springs of emotion and was long remembered in the region. Unlike some, his devotion to the Carolina Low Country was not restricted to his own class and kind, but, with a strong and tender compassion, embraced the black slaves as an impelling, personal priority. His depth of commitment and the response it won in the heart of a vast host of slaves throughout the Low Country could only be explained by the beautiful work of the Spirit of God in an imperfect, but sincere and consecrated heart. Although from our late twentieth-century perspective, his desire to serve the blacks was not purged from a definitely paternalistic attitude we must ask ourselves whether we are fair to expect anything else from his time and place.

12

A UNIQUE MINISTRY TO LOW COUNTRY BLACKS

We must now say more about Girardeau's fruitful and lengthy ministry to the black people of South Carolina. This is, as I have already indicated, at the forefront of his spiritual legacy to us today, and merits appreciative consideration. For one thing, because we here consider Girardeau as a Reformed preacher, we must note that his greatest and most effective and anointed preaching was without doubt that which he delivered to the black people. But before we can look at the precise nature of his preaching to the blacks, we must mention the shape of his ecclesiastical relationship to them, and then briefly glance at the closing years of his ministry. From that vantage point we may survey in considerable detail the style, content and results of his preaching.

By the mid-nineteenth century, it was generally recognized that the black population in the Upper Country of South Carolina had far more privileges of hearing the gospel than those in the less populous Low Country, where there was a great deal more ignorance and practice of Voodoo. Thus, Girardeau's heart had turned to his native Low Country with its slave population which beckoned to him as a desperately needy mission field as well as being his true spiritual home. Without going into minor details, we may note that the Second Presbyterian Church of Charleston (which Girardeau had attended as a schoolboy) started a new mission congregation in the early 1850s for a number of their black members, which was known as the Anson Street Mission. At the same time, Girardeau was proving himself a highly effective preacher and pastor to the black slave community around the Wilton Church in rural Colleton County, where he regularly preached to a large congregation of whites in the morning and blacks in the afternoon, not to mention systematic preaching visitations to the slaves on the surrounding plantations.

This is how Girardeau in later years described his sense of mission to the Low Country black people and his mode of ministering to them just before he was called to Charleston as pastor of the newly formed church at Anson Street:

> While at the Theological Seminary, I only refrained from going on a foreign mission, because I felt it to be my duty to preach to the mass of slaves on the seaboard of South Carolina. Having rejected, after licensure, a call to a large and important church which had very few negroes connected with it, I accepted an invitation to preach temporarily to a small church which was surrounded by a dense body of slaves. The scenes on Sabbath were affecting. The negroes came in crowds from two parishes. Often have I seen (a sight, I reckon, not often witnessed) groups of them 'double-quicking' in the roads, in order to reach the church in time – trotting to church!
>
> The white service, as many negroes as could attending, being over, the slaves would pour in and throng the seats vacated by their masters – yes, cram the building up to the pulpit. I have seen them rock to and fro, under the influence of their feelings, like a wood in a storm. What singing! What hearty handshakings after the service! I have had my finger joints stripped of the scarfskin in consequence of them.
>
> Upon leaving the church after the last, mournful service with them, and going to my vehicle, which was some hundred yards distant, a poor little native African woman followed me weeping and crying out, 'O Massa, you goin' to leave us? O Massa, for Jesus' sake, don't leave us!' I had made an engagement with another church, or the poor little African's plea might have prevailed. When next I visited that people, I asked after my little African friend. 'She crossed over, sir,' was the answer. May we meet where parting will be no more, the song to Jesus never cease![12]

Girardeau describes the wrenching emotion of his last preaching service with these people so near to his heart:

> My last service with the negroes at his church I will never forget. The final words had been spoken to the white congregation, and they had retired. While a tempest of emotion was shaking me behind the desk, the tramp of a great multitude was heard as the negroes poured into the building, and occupied all available space up to the little old

wine-glass shaped pulpit. When approaching the conclusion of the sermon, I turned to the unconverted, asked what I should say to *them*, and called on them to come to Jesus. At this moment the great mass of the congregation simultaneously broke down, dropped their heads to their knees, and uttered a wail which seemed to prelude the judgment. Poor people! They had deeply appreciated the preaching of the Gospel to them.[13]

From these rural scenes, Girardeau moved to the heart of busy Charleston, as pastor of the new black mission church at Anson Street. In 1854, when he came, there were thirty-six members, but by 1860 there were over six hundred official members, with a regular Sunday attendance of fifteen hundred. While the church was largely black, perhaps ten percent or more of its membership consisted of sympathetic whites. As the church grew rapidly under Girardeau's preaching, a much larger building was erected for the vast congregation of Calhoun Street (called Zion Church). It, in fact, was the largest church building – for any race or denomination – in Charleston, and possibly in all of South Carolina.

We speak today of the Church Growth philosophy, of ethnic ministries, of innovative approaches to congregational life, of a needed emphasis on body life and the development of lay leadership, of effective sessional shepherding of the flock, of 'Evangelism Explosion', 'The Church Unleashed' and so forth. Hopefully, we have learned something from all of these approaches. Yet, in a certain sense, we might say that John L. Girardeau was far ahead of his time in that he was doing some things in his ministry at Zion Church which would now be considered the latest ministerial innovation or avant-garde desideratum! The surprising thing is that this man was a conservative of conservatives in the Calvinist camp. Had you asked him why he would decide to strike out in an unusual direction, his answer would have been simple: he was merely returning to the scriptural practicalities of true Presbyterian government and was following in the train of the Genevan and Scottish reformations.

Where he was so remarkably innovative, and with such stupendous results (given the paternalist, slave mentality of the ruling class at that time), was in his development of highly effective spiritual and pastoral leadership among his black, slave laity. In addition to the normal pattern at Zion of powerful preaching and a powerful prayer meeting (though the spiritual unction was far above the normal), he took the unusual step of dividing the entire congregation into classes, which would not exceed fifty in number. When the class grew beyond this, it would be divided by the session, under whose authority all of the classes operated. There was an appropriate lay leader at the head of each class with an assistant lay leader, who, if he proved himself, might later become the head of his own class. The purpose of these class meetings was stated in Rule 7 of the Zion bylaws:

> The objects of the class meetings are – to promote mutual acquaintance and brotherly love among the members; to apprise them of one another's sickness and need; to acquaint the leaders with the same; and to further the growth of the members in Christian knowledge and experimental religion.[14]

These class meetings also ministered to the needs of the body, since applications for aid on behalf of sick and needy members were to be made through the class leaders, who met each Monday night to discuss these matters after the prayer meeting. A weekly stipend of fifty cents was to be appropriated to each sick member as long as the class leaders deemed it needful. It is reasonable to assume that Girardeau may have learned something along these lines from the eighteenth-century Wesleyan Methodist class-meetings, but this cannot be ascertained. A more certain influence on Girardeau's procedure was the great Thomas Chalmers, leader of the 1843 Disruption of the Church of Scotland, who had done strategic work in socially disadvantaged parishes in industrialized Scotland during the early nineteenth century – such as in his own St John's parish in Glasgow. Dr Thomas Smyth, former pastor of Girardeau, and still pastor of the Second Presbyterian Church of Charleston, which was the sponsoring 'mother' church of Zion, had visited Chalmers just after the Disruption, and had seen first-hand Chalmers' organization of parishes such as St John's.[15] Certainly Girardeau's shepherding developed spiritual maturity, economic responsibility and general strength of character among the laity of the antebellum Zion Presbyterian Church on Calhoun Street.

As is well known, there was an outbreak of revival in the United States in 1857 and 1858, which then also occurred in Great Britain in 1858 and 1859. This movement of the Spirit was unlike some previous revivals in that it did not affect a whole geographical region, but rather seemed to jump from area to area. Wherever it did touch down, however, there was a great tide of faith and repentance, sorrow and joy, regeneration and conversion, restoration and reformation. It was just such a work of God that broke out in Zion Church after a long season of congregational prayer in 1858:

This began with a prayer meeting that constantly increased until the house was filled. Some of the officers of the church wanted him to commence preaching services, but he steadily refused, waiting for the outpouring of the Spirit. His view was that the Father had given to Jesus, as the King and Head of the church, the gift of the Holy Spirit, and that Jesus in His sovereign administration of the affairs of His church, bestowed Him upon whomsoever He pleased, and in whatever measure He pleased. Day after day he, therefore, kept his prayer addressed directly to the mediatorial throne for the Holy Spirit in mighty reviving power.

One evening, while leading the people in prayer, he received a sensation as if a bolt of electricity had struck his head and diffused itself through his whole body. For a little while he stood speechless under the strange physical feeling. Then he said: 'The Holy Spirit has come; we will begin preaching tomorrow evening.' He closed the service with a hymn, dismissed the congregation, and came down from the pulpit; but no one left the house. The whole congregation had quietly resumed its seat. Instantly he realized the situation. The Holy Spirit had not only come to him – He had also taken possession of the hearts of the people. Immediately he began exhorting them to accept the Gospel. They began to sob, softly, like the falling of rain; then, with deeper emotion, to weep bitterly, or to rejoice loudly, according to their circumstances. It was midnight before he could dismiss his congregation . . . The meeting went on night and day for eight weeks. Large numbers of both white and black were converted and joined the various churches of the city. His own was wonderfully built up, not only in numbers, but also in an experience that remained in the church. He was accustomed to say that he could always count on those who were converted in that meeting. This was probably due to the deep work of conviction of sin, the protracted period of the conviction, the clear sense of pardon, and the joyful witness of the Spirit to their adoption.[16]

Let it be added here that, unlike the Arminian revivalist, Finney, Girardeau knew that revival could not be worked up by man through any combination of spiritual techniques; it had to be sent down from heaven. Some years after the War Between the States, Girardeau and his old Zion congregation (the remnant of it which remained) organized sunrise prayer meetings to seek revival. This continued for over a year, yet nothing spectacular happened. Dr Girardeau wisely and simply said: 'God is a sovereign.'

The structure of Girardeau's busy pastoral life changed radically with the outbreak of the War Between the States in 1861. He was convinced that the Southern case was right and that the basic issue was a defense of the constitutional liberties of a formerly conservative, decentralized republic, now on the verge of being turned into a liberal, secular, centralized democracy. Obviously, Christians in the North read the issues very differently, and of course their interpretation (as the victors) is the one generally accepted by historians. Our concern in any case will not be to discuss the complex causes of the war, but merely to mention Girardeau's Christian ministry during that terrible conflict.

He served throughout the war as chaplain of the Twenty-third Regiment of the South Carolina Volunteers. He saw some of the worst fighting around Petersburg, Virginia; we hear of him in Mississippi at the fall of Vicksburg, as well as in Georgia and the Carolinas. Confederate though he was, his Christ-like compassion for the hurting and dying was not limited to his own fellow Southern soldiers. On more than one occasion he knelt down beside wounded and dying Yankee soldiers, praying for them and ministering to them as best he could.

After the war, Girardeau returned to a defeated, depressed, trauma-ridden Charleston, and took pastoral charge again of the remnants of his dwindling congregation. The situation was vastly changed – legally, socially, economically and culturally – and would never be the same. Many of the black Christians felt it now inappropriate to be under a white pastor, though a large number did soon return to his ministrations. The relationship between black and white in the South would be changed not only by the defensiveness and bitterness of many of the Southern whites, but also by the specific policy of the victorious

Northern government's Freedman Bureau, which was to divide the black free citizens from the Southern white populace (in order to divide and conquer). This bureau strongly encouraged the blacks to leave the white churches and to form their own with help from the Washington government. It actually took over the Zion (Calhoun Street) church building, so the congregation had to meet elsewhere.

It is fully understandable that large numbers of black Christians would be only too glad to find at last a 'breathing space' from the paternalist white leadership over every sphere of their lives. They did so by drawing apart from the white denominational structures in order to align themselves with already existing black denominations, where they could develop and exercise their own leadership and their own rich approach to spirituality and worship. The refusal of white ecclesiastical judicatories to allow the freed black Christians to become elders and deacons (as in Robert L. Dabney's famous, controversial speech on this subject in the Synod of Virginia during the 1870s) ensured a growing exodus of blacks from the white denominations. This kind of segregation had not existed in that form in the church before, so, while it is definite that many Southerners would soon welcome this trend, it is only fair to say that Northerners as well as Southerners had a hand in the deeply changing relationships between the two races.

13

CHANGES AFTER THE CIVIL WAR: A PROFESSORSHIP AND PASTORATE IN COLUMBIA

This change in racial relationships had its effects upon Girardeau's post-war ministry. Although he maintained his lifelong zeal for the spiritual well-being of the black population, owing to the changed sociological conditions, his pre-war ministry was no longer practicable, and he served until the mid 1870s as pastor of a largely (though not totally) white congregation in Charleston. His post-war congregation raised remarkable sums of money for world missions, sustained many struggling Presbyterian churches throughout Low Country South Carolina, and organized several mission Sabbath schools (including one for the blacks) in various parts of Charleston.

Throughout these years Girardeau had become increasingly well known across the South as both a great preacher and a profound scholar. The latter is perhaps surprising in light of his studied efforts always to make himself intelligible to the simplest servants in his Low Country congregations. Although he was quietly self-effacing, his gifts and graces had become widely known and appreciated. Thus he was elected moderator of the General Assembly of the (Southern) Presbyterian Church in 1874. His moderatorial address delivered at the following General Assembly in 1875 showed that he was not one to attempt to curry favor by accommodating himself to the spirit of the age. This address was on the Puritan regulative principle of Scripture in which Girardeau maintained that any usage of instrumental music in public worship was not commanded and therefore not properly allowed by the Word of

God. While large numbers disagreed with his position, he had obviously maintained their respect, for that same assembly elected him as Professor of Didactic and Polemic Theology in Columbia Theological Seminary. He was most hesitant to accept this post for which he considered himself unqualified, yet the following year he relented and left Charleston for Columbia, where he would remain until the close of his life some twenty-two years later.

I shall give a much less detailed description of Girardeau's professorial career than of his previous pastorates simply because it ran in much more traditional channels than his pastoral ministry and because its details are far less essential to an understanding of his preaching, to which theme we must soon turn. Earlier in this chapter we have dealt with the general theological orientation of Girardeau and of the Southern Presbyterian tradition. That needs no repetition here. He held a high view of the Westminster standards and believed a strict subscription to them should be required of ministers and elders.[17] He felt further that a professor in the seminary should not teach anything that ran contrary to the standards, and thus when his colleague, Dr James Woodrow (uncle of President Woodrow Wilson) began teaching the theory of organic evolution at Columbia, Girardeau opposed him, and in fact withdrew from the seminary for a year until Woodrow was dismissed in the mid-1880s. Then Girardeau felt free to return and he remained until he was seventy years of age in 1895. He then retired after some nineteen years of theological teaching.

For his senior theology class, Girardeau chose Charles Hodge's work as the main textbook, with much required reading in Calvin's *Institutes*, Turretin, Thornwell's volume II, and others. He also had his classes read widely in those areas of philosophy which touch true religion; indeed, much of his best effort in his later years was expended here. He had carried the writings of Jonathan Edwards '*On the Will*' with him through the war, and produced a significant volume on this subject as well as valuable volumes on *Theological Questions*, *Philosophical Questions* and a book against instrumental music in the church. Girardeau stayed firmly in the line of Southern Presbyterian Calvinism and Scottish Common Sense Realism, though he was an independent thinker who was prepared, when he deemed it necessary, to disagree with Edwards, Hodge, Dabney and others. All his theological and philosophical writings combine the twofold Southern Presbyterian attributes which we have mentioned earlier: high intellectual endeavor along with precision and heartfelt, revival Christianity.

His Columbia colleague, W. T. Hall, with some insight, assessed the professorate of Girardeau in relation to others:

> History teaches that several conditions must meet in order to the production of a great theologian. Chief among these are extraordinary endowments, both natural and gracious; prolonged occupation as a professional instructor, and the stimulus of some absorbing religious crisis. This statement might be illustrated by referring to Calvin and Chalmers, or to Hodge, Dabney and Thornwell in our own country. The first and third of these conditions met in the case of Dr. Girardeau, but the second was, in a measure absent. He entered the Seminary as a teacher in January, 1876, and retired voluntarily, as he began to feel the burden of years in May, 1895. Time enough was allowed to form an acquaintance with the broad field of theology and its kindred sciences, but not for formulating the result in a systematic treatise. His pen was not idle . . . but his published works are critical rather than constructive.[18]

There is another way to look at this absence of a systematic theology, however. Thornton Whaling, Girardeau's student, who later taught in the seminary, wisely suggests that providentially Girardeau's attention was given to certain important philosophical questions (such as the will and sovereignty) and theological questions (such as the meaning of adoption, of the place of deacons, and some aspects of federal headship), which needed developing with a richness of detail that could not very likely have happened had Girardeau devoted himself to producing another nineteenth-century systematic theology. Moreover, I would add as one who has served as both pastor and professor, that his pastoral background would have given a depth, richness, sweetness and power to his teaching. In my opinion, his teaching would have been less valuable to his students in his maturer years, if he had spent the earlier part of his life in a library and classroom instead of at Charleston – but of course, the sovereign Master leads different men differently.

We may conclude our brief overview of his theological professorate with this prayer which he wrote at the end of his first day of teaching theology at Columbia, on January 18, 1876:

I commit myself and this work to which I did *not* call myself, to the Almighty, faithful hands of the Lord Jesus. Glorious Savior! I adore, I admire, I love Thee! Use me to show forth Thy matchless beauty, loveliness and glory! Enrich me with all knowledge and utterance, for Thy name's sake. Amen. J.L.G.[19]

During the year in which he withdrew from Columbia Seminary owing to the Woodrow evolutionary controversy, Girardeau had a hand in organizing a new and important congregation in downtown Columbia. It was first called Second Presbyterian Church, but has long since been known as Arsenal Hill Church. He accepted the pastorate of this church under the conditions that no instrumental music or choirs be allowed and that the members should not frequent card parties and dances. We shall later note that an important element of his preaching in his later years was against worldliness and materialism, which he perceived to be entering the churches in the more liberalized and secularizing, post-Reconstruction society of the United States. While few of us now would draw the lines exactly where he did, who of us could honestly deny that the church is far less concerned for holiness today than it was in times of revival and reformation?

A touching scene that occurred in Girardeau's last year of life in the Arsenal Hill Church must close our discussion of his life as minister and professor. It occurred during a visit from his old friend from Confederate chaplain days, Dr Robert L. Dabney, a fellow Southern Presbyterian theologian of the first rank:

When . . . Dr. Dabney, himself afflicted with blindness, heard of the partial paralysis of his friend, he came to Columbia to visit him. Their communion was sweet, and in a measure the spirit of other days seemed to come back on them. On Sunday, Dr. Dabney preached to a large congregation, in the Arsenal Hill Church, on the power of love. The sermon was one of extraordinary power, and when he came in his discourse to the love of Jesus for his aged servants many in the congregation were weeping. Dr. Girardeau himself was deeply moved, while the hearty congregational singing, unaccompanied by any instrument of music, seemed to greatly affect Dr. Dabney.

When the service was over the two came down the aisle together; they were men of imposing presence, each like the son of a king; their faces showed the influence of chastening grace; their foreheads betokened the might of the intellects behind them; venerable men! dignity, goodness, and greatness sat with ease and naturalness upon them. Dr. Girardeau said: 'Doctor, that was a glorious sermon this morning.' Dr. Dabney replied, 'This has been a sweet service to me, and this singing carries me back to old Tinkling Spring.' Dr. Girardeau said: 'But what will it be in heaven?' The answer of Dr. Dabney was lost in the tramping of the congregation. And so, blind and lame these princes in Israel walked on, talking of the past and future worship of God. A few months after this meeting they both joined the general assembly of the church of the first born in the majestic worship of their God and Savior.[20]

14

GIRARDEAU THE PREACHER

Girardeau had a profound grasp of the Reformed faith and was skilled in preaching it with unusual power, clarity and unction to the men and women of his own culture. His preaching, like his theology and practice, combined what we have termed the twin Southern Presbyterian attributes of informed, precise Calvinism on the one hand, and soul-stirring revival Christianity on the other. Dr B. M. Palmer, who, as we have seen, must be ranked as one of the greatest of all American preachers of any age, confirms my assessment of this rare combination of qualities in Girardeau's preaching. In a letter of condolence to Girardeau's widow on July 5, 1898, he speaks of her husband in these words:

> . . . endowed with royal intellectual gifts, these were equaled if not surpassed by the qualities of his heart. Indeed, the combination of natural and moral attributes was exceedingly rare and stamped him with an individuality altogether his own. A physical nervous force, like an electric current, ran along the line of his vigorous thought as well as through his deep emotional nature, to constitute him one of the greatest of our modern preachers. Better than all, his fervent piety and deep religious experience, gave a holy sanction to all his public teaching.[21]

It was undoubtedly this combination of qualities which caused Girardeau's preaching to be rated so highly by his contemporaries – in tones of praise which, to those who never heard him, sound exaggerated. When he was only thirty-five, a knowledgeable peer described his preaching to a young student from Georgia:

My first meeting with Dr. Girardeau was in 1860 at the residence of Rev. Dr. John B. Adger, while I was a student in the Columbia Theological Seminary. Pointing to Dr. Girardeau, who was on the other side of the room, Dr. Adger emphatically affirmed to several of us, 'There is the Spurgeon of America, the grandest preacher in all of our Southland.' This statement then seemed to me a very extravagant one, and provoked the criticism, 'See how these South Carolinians love one another.' But afterwards I often realized that it was strictly and entirely true.[22]

In the 1880s, the Rev. J. M. Buckley, a distinguished Northern Methodist scholar and editor of the *New York Christian Advocate*, happened to be passing through Columbia, South Carolina, one weekend, and asked who was the best preacher in the city. He was directed to Arsenal Hill Presbyterian Church, where Dr. Girardeau was preaching. These reactions were later reported by Dr. Buckley in his New York magazine:

I have now to say that, having heard Thomas Guthrie of Edinburgh, James Hamilton of London, and Mr. Spurgeon six or eight times, it has never fallen to my lot to hear a more absorbing spiritual, eloquent and moving sermon on an ordinary occasion. It was worthy of William Wirt's Blind Preacher. It made all the preaching I have ever done, and nearly all I have ever heard seem like mere sermonizing. Looking around to catch the eye of my friend, I saw that two-thirds of all the men in the audience were in tears. It was no rant or artificial excitement or mere pathos, but *thought* burning and glowing. None but a man of equal intellect, learning, piety and eloquence could preach such a discourse without notes.[23]

In 1881 during the Columbia Seminary centennial celebration, Dr W. A. Wood of Statesville, North Carolina, Dr James H. Thornwell, Jr (son of the famous theologian) and Dr Joseph Mack were part of a congregation enthralled by Girardeau's sermon on the ascension of Christ. This is their report:

For the first half hour, with logic on fire, he discussed an important doctrine, and then described its glorious effects, closing with a vivid view of our Savior's ascension and the descent of the angelic hosts meeting Him with song and the chimes of silver cymbals. As he began to close almost every hearer was either leaning forward or else was standing up, and as after he ceased to speak he continued to move his hands in circles up, and up, and up, stopping for a second at the completion of each circle, the sweet chimes of silver cymbals in angel hands seemed to fill the house and thrill every heart.

For over a minute all remained spellbound and breathless, and then came the rustling sound as they fell back into their seats like those wakening from a delightful dream. No prayer was made, no hymn was sung, only the benediction was pronounced, and then in silence the strangely impressed hearers quietly passed out of the church.

Dr. Wood, Dr. J. H. Thornwell, Jr. of Fort Mill, and myself (Dr. Joseph Mack) were together. Not a word was spoken until nearly a square had we gone. I broke the silence by saying, 'Brother Wood, you have now heard Dr. Girardeau, and what do you think?' Clasping his hands together and looking upward, he replied, 'It was more than magnificent. I have never heard anything to equal that. No other man can speak like that man.' Dr. Thornwell then added in a voice trembling with emotion, 'Put me down for $100.00 to the endowment of the Seminary as a thank offering for the privilege of hearing that sermon. It is worth ten times that much to me in my work, but that is all I have to give.'[24]

Girardeau's Christ-centered, soul-searching preaching could move congregations of the famous and influential as well as his own beloved Low Country blacks. Even General Robert E. Lee (then President of Washington and Lee College in Lexington, Virginia) is said to have made no attempt to hide his overflowing emotion at a sermon that Girardeau preached on prayer at the college in 1869.[25] Several years earlier, just before the war broke out, General Butler was in Charleston at the National Democratic Convention. This general, who was so soon to lead Northern troops against the Confederacy, attended Girardeau's preaching to the black congregation in Zion Church, Calhoun Street. Colonel Alfred Robb, a lawyer from Middle Tennessee, who was with General Butler, gives this impression of the occasion:

The sermon was tender and spiritual, and though profound, was plain, delivered with fire and unction. After the preacher took his seat, deeply impressed, I was with closed eyes meditating on the wonderful sermon, when I heard someone sobbing. Looking around I saw General Butler's face bathed in tears. Just then the church officers came for the usual collection and at once General Butler drew from his pockets both hands full of silver coin (put there to tip the waiters), and cast it into the basket, with the audible remark, 'Well, I have never heard such a man and have never heard such a sermon.'[26]

Many years later, Girardeau was called to preach before the Legislature of South Carolina, and they specifically requested that he preach his sermon on 'The Last Judgment.' R. A. Webb tells us:

He did so in the First Presbyterian Church of Columbia. A great congregation was present, crowding both the floor and galleries, which were then on three sides of the building. The preacher was fully up to himself, in voice, gesture and spirit. Contrary to his general custom, he delivered it from the manuscript. It was an hour and a half long. Attention was tense from the first. But when the flute-like voice rose to its best, reinforced by the silent language of gesture and face, many of the hearers stretched themselves forward as far as they could reach. Tears poured down cheeks and spittle fell from relaxed mouths. When the preacher's voice hushed the multitude fell back into position with an audible heave, which sounded as if it had come simultaneously from every breast.[27]

Of even greater significance than generals, legislatures and academic audiences in assessing the greatness of Girardeau's preaching would be the touched hearts and changed lives of thousands of nameless black people in the Low Country of this state. But we shall come to the character and effects of his preaching on the blacks presently.

Before we discuss the peculiarities of his mode of preaching to black congregations, let us first look in a general way at his preaching style and pulpit demeanor.

From contemporary reports, there was a definite difference about Girardeau's type of preaching, a quality that was nearly impossible to describe. One of his old Glebe Street Church members of Charleston wrote in 1898:

As a preacher Dr. Girardeau was *sui generis*. His style was his own, and what that style was those who heard him in his prime can testify. The most abstract discussion, under the fire of his earnestness and desire to convince, became luminous. Hence he was never dull. His application and peroration were often masterpieces of impassioned eloquence. All his gifts of oratory, all the stores of learning he had treasured up in his well disciplined mind he laid as a tribute at his Master's feet. The pathos, the tender appeal, the solemn warning, the tone of voice, the graceful gesture, the eye, now flashing with the fervor of his thought, now melting into tenderness – these are simply indescribable.[28]

Perhaps part of this indescribable 'something' was the way Girardeau apparently unconsciously threw the totality of his whole being – body and soul – into the act of preaching God's living, burning truth. This whole-soul aspect of his preaching comes to the fore in a description of his pulpit powers at the age of forty:

He was a man of superb physique, tall (about five feet ten or eleven inches), rather slender at this time, though he grew stouter as age advanced; muscular, agile and with fine use of his body in every way. And in the pulpit his action was energetic, graceful and exceedingly impressive – a gesture often thrilling the hearer. His voice was keen and penetrating, but, at the same time, smooth and musical. His mind was quick and logical, with well trained faculties and strongly disposed to reading and study. His taste was poetic – he often composed beautiful hymns – his imagination vivid, and his descriptive powers wonderful. His temperament was ardent and his emotions strong.

His demeanor in the pulpit was dignified, grave and earnest, indicating that he fully realized his responsibility as an ambassador of Christ and a minister to dying men. I can never forget the solemn countenance he carried into the pulpit and the earnestness with which he read the hymns and conducted the services. And he threw his whole self, body, mind and spirit, into his preaching, speaking with a fervor such as I have rarely seen equalled in the pulpit, and which deeply impressed his hearers with his zeal for God and for their souls.[29]

Other descriptions make us think that he must have been somewhat like the great evangelist, George Whitefield, with that rare and wonderful combination of physical, intellectual, emotional, vocal and spiritual powers which blend together to make a mighty orator. Girardeau's son-in-law speaks of his flute-like voice, his gestures and his consummate ability to command the English language:

His figure was tall, straight, well-proportioned and athletic; his movements were easy and graceful; his face was strong, and his blue eyes could beam with love or flash with fire as occasion required; his voice was full, rich and sweet; it was said that when preaching in the early days of his ministry, it sounded like the notes of a flute; it certainly had wonderful compass; he could make it imitate the lapping of the water on the beach, the roll of distant thunder, or anything else for which his high-wrought and splendid rhetoric called; his gestures, always made unconsciously, were strong and impressive and exactly suited to impress the thought that he wished to convey.[30]

Yet having said all of this, we are still, I fear, far from capturing the thrilling, gripping power of Girardeau's pulpit ministrations. We must finally say of Girardeau's preaching what George Whitefield said of his own sermons when someone asked permission to print them in Philadelphia: 'Well, I have no inherent objection, if you like, but you will never be able to put on the printed page the lightning and the thunder.'[31] Probably the closest we can come to describing that indescribable 'something' and capturing that elusive thunder and lightning in Girardeau's preaching is to imagine ourselves stealing silently across the years back into the old black congregations of Low Country, where Girardeau's heart always remained. Many competent observers believed that it was to the blacks that Girardeau did his very finest, most inspired preaching. The famous periodical, *The Christian Observer*, said:

Among the last comments he ever made upon himself was: 'I could preach to the negroes. That's about all I was ever fit for.' No one who never heard him preach to the negroes ever heard him at his best. To them he talked as an angel from the skies. To them he preached on the profoundest problems of religion, and discussed the most intricate questions of Christian experience. It seemed to me that before an audience of negroes he could make the doctrine of the Trinity plain.[32]

In this regard, incidentally, *The Christian Observer* answers a question that may have occurred to the reader before now: If Girardeau was so great, and was even fifty percent as eloquent as Spurgeon, then why has the world never heard of him? *The Observer* gives us a clue:

Men of culture, some of them distinguished preachers, who had heard Guthrie, Candlish, Cunningham, James Hamilton, French, Cumming, and Spurgeon, have declared that Girardeau excelled them all. But he always depreciated himself as a preacher, and for this reason, while he met his appointments at home, it was difficult to induce him to preach elsewhere. The world consequently never came to know him.[33]

In other words, he chose to pour out his heart and energies on an underprivileged people in a relatively remote corner of the world's great stage. His failure to achieve the world-wide fame his preaching deserved must be attributed to two main considerations. First, in his earlier ministry he was deeply identified with poor, slave people, who were often despised, and secondly, during his later ministry he was tarred with the brush of a defeated Confederacy, which closed not a few doors to him in the wider world. Added to these factors was his deliberate choice not to write out most of his sermons, so that unlike Spurgeon in London and Palmer in New Orleans (both of whom permitted stenographers), little would have been available for newspapers or periodicals to publish regularly. Probably a large part of his reason for declining to write out sermons was his studious concern in his younger years to communicate with the slave population in a vital, direct way. But if his relative obscurity be considered a loss, it is the kind of loss that for the believer in Jesus is gain; it is the kind of death to selfish and worldly considerations from which Christ's resurrection power flows out to raise others into newness of life.

Girardeau's preaching was just that for many Low Country black people: life from the dead. Unless I am mistaken, the clue to Girardeau's exceptional preaching rapport with the antebellum blacks will be found in a central theological concept closely related to this death to self which we have just noted: there must be an incarnation of ourselves in the lives and therefore culture of those to whom we seek to minister. For some years now cross-cultural missionaries have spoken to us of the central necessity of an 'incarnational' theology and practice for fruitful missionary endeavor. One must immerse oneself in the different patterns of a strange culture in order genuinely to incarnate the love of Jesus to those people. That is exactly what Girardeau did. He knew death to self on behalf of others.

The incarnational testimony of Girardeau was beautifully illustrated before the War Between the States, when one of his black members was questioned by a fellow black as to why he attended a church with a white pastor. His reply was, 'Yas, he

[sic] face is white, but he heart is black.'[34] Because he so loved these people, he worked hard to communicate in a way that they could understand. He did such a superb job of communicating with the blacks, in fact, that some whites felt themselves left behind. One such observer writes:

Sometimes when both races were present he would preach a profound sermon, and there would be witnessed a strange anomaly. The minds of the cultured whites would be strained to keep up with the train of thought, while the negroes seemed to clearly understand and fully appreciate the whole sermon. Hence the remark was frequently made, 'How can those ignorant negroes understand such a sermon?'

Being myself much perplexed, I asked him to explain the problem. He replied, 'The negroes understand my sermon as clearly but not as fully as you do. I have acquired the power to put *key-words* in my sentences, and to emphasize them both in tone and by manner, and as they are vividly impressed by those words they secure the current of my thought.'

To illustrate this: He preached a sermon in which the first part was on the vileness of sin and the certainty of its punishment. There was the phrase 'Holy God' spoken in a tone of deep humility and awe – then 'sin hateful,' with a look of intense abhorrence – then 'God angry' with an expression of heartfelt indignation, and then among other words were 'judge,' 'guilty,' 'doomed,' 'death,' 'hell,' 'wailing,' 'forever,' and each word or phrase so emphasized in tone and by gesture as to stamp its meaning upon the mind of the hearer. One could easily see how, through such word painting, the ignorant hearer could readily grasp the main line of truth, and without any weakening of its power by trying also to lay hold upon the subordinate thoughts connected with it. The negro got enough to fill his head and heart, not too much as to overflow and bring confusion to his mind.[35]

We must not fail to see that Girardeau's preaching methodology was not developed 'out of thin air'; rather, it was based upon an important presupposition he held, with which not all of his peers would have necessarily agreed. Not only did black slaves have souls which needed to be saved, he also believed they had intelligent minds which were capable of assimilating and doing great things with the truth of God. One of his ministerial colleagues in the presbytery of Charleston said this: 'He would listen with profound respect to the humblest negroes, and cheerfully acknowledged that from them he had often learned some of the profoundest and most important lessons of the Christian life.'[36]

In addition to his apt usage of 'key words' his vivid imagination and ability to paint both beautiful and arresting word pictures riveted the attention of his audiences on the message. Moreover, throughout his sermons he gave clear calls to cast oneself on the saving mercy of Christ in ways that sinners of every class could understand. We shall return to both of these qualities presently, when we discuss the structure of his preaching.

15

EXALTING AND PROCLAIMING CHRIST

Having considered the special nature of Girardeau's preaching to the slave culture of South Carolina, we must now move to a broader view of the totality of his lifetime of preaching, to both black and white. First to be considered is the content of his preaching, then its structure, its effects and its source of power.

What the Apostle Paul said of the content of his own preaching at Corinth can without the least exaggeration be said of Girardeau's fifty years of preaching: 'For I determined not to know any thing among you, save Jesus Christ, and him crucified' (1 Cor. 2:2). A colleague, who knew Girardeau's preaching well, said this:

> To preach Jesus Christ and Him crucified was the 'one thing' of his life, his chiefest joy – and often did the tones of his voice so reveal this highest delight of his heart as to make the melody of his words sound as sweetly as the echoes of the morning.[37]

While Girardeau's preaching from first to last was Christocentric, it was not at the expense of the other sacred persons of the Godhead. His preaching was based on a solid Reformed theological structure, in which he brought his people face to face in the most vital way with the overarching realities of the Holy Trinity; the two natures of Christ in one person; eternal election; sovereign grace; justification by faith; the necessary struggles of sanctification; the sweet spirit of adoption; the certainty of the perseverance of the saints; and the bright future of God's people – all these truths and others stated in relationship to the major goal of existence, the greater glory of

God. Not a few observers expressed surprise at the theological nature of his preaching to the black slaves, and even greater surprise at the fruit it bore.

Within this context of thoroughly evangelical Calvinist orthodoxy, we note some key themes and emphases particularly prominent in Girardeau's preaching throughout the years. The atonement of Christ was always a major theme of his proclamation, and often entire congregations were broken down as he displayed with sweetness and power the 'mingled love and sorrow' of the eternal Son of God dying for sinners on Calvary's hill. Sad to say, the finest of his sermons on this constant theme were all unwritten, though his surviving sermon on John 12:24, 'The Dying Corn of Wheat and its Glorious Harvest' gives us a little glimpse of his approach.[38] Here is an instance of his presentation of the Man of the cross to his congregation, as reported by a hearer:

Once in Zion (Calhoun Street) Church of Charleston, he was preaching to a large congregation of negroes. As in plaintive tones he pictured Jesus Christ going forth to death and bending beneath the burden of the cross, every eye was opened wide and riveted upon the speaker, while each breast seemed to rise and fall, as step after step was taken up the rugged steep of Calvary. When the place of execution was reached everybody fell back and many hands were raised in horror. When the nails were driven a deep sigh swept through the house like the sad moan of the sea as it rolls in upon the shore, and when the Savior's head was dropped in death a deep shudder convulsed the weeping throng as hundreds piteously cried, 'O, my God! O, my God!'[39]

When, as a professor in his later years, he was asked for advice on how to choose suitable subjects for preaching, he emphasized the importance of adhering to the proclamation of the gospel in one's ministry. In some class notes preserved by one of his students on the theme of eschatology, Girardeau gave this advice about preaching on the end of time:

The peculiar nature of the subject makes it necessary that one should guard himself against the danger of making it a hobby. What! The relative importance of the Priestly and Kingly functions of Christ. The former constitute the *great theme* of the preacher – Christ crucified. If we are to magnify any one department of revealed truth, above others, let it be that which is concerned about atonement, the way of Life to the perishing sinner.[40]

Girardeau goes on to state that the kingly office of Christ is important and should be preached, but with careful balance, 'according to the analogy of Scripture.'

Allied to and flowing from his great theme of atonement is his stress on the need of definite conversion. He did not hesitate to emphasize the urgency of coming to Christ as personal Lord and Savior. It is interesting to note that after the turn of the century, apparently many Southern Presbyterian churches lost this sense of urgency. Thus, whether rightly or wrongly, the popular conception has been that in the twentieth century it has been the Baptist Church and various parachurch groups which have been most concerned about evangelism.

There is probably an element of truth here, for, as the Southern Presbyterian Church became increasingly liberal, it certainly did relax soul-winning efforts. Dr Morton Smith, in his article on 'Southern Presbyterian Theology,' points out that in the early years of Reformed Theological Seminary, there was a great deal of serious and earnest discussion of proper methods of evangelism, which of course indicated a renewed zeal for evangelism among Presbyterians in the South.[41] Not unexpectedly, this renewed passion for reaching the lost for Christ came precisely from those elements in the Southern church who were theologically minded in a decidedly Calvinist direction. After all, this is as it should be, granted that Girardeau, one of our fathers in the faith, was such a powerful evangelistic preacher directly because of his Reformed theology. For example, the following was said of his preaching and ministrations to the Confederate wounded and dying at the Battle of Jackson, Mississippi:

> . . . there I could note the tenderness and faithfulness of his ministrations, as he held up Christ crucified as the only hope of a sinner. All his preaching that I heard in the army, was full of appeal to men to accept Christ and trust him for life or death.[42]

Listen also to an eyewitness account of Girardeau pleading with sinners to come to Jesus. The place is Whippy Swamp in the backwoods of Low Country, South Carolina, and the year 1870:

In a voice tremulous with emotion he tenderly told them of their critical, their very critical condition because of the presence of God's Holy Spirit, and pointed to Christ as a refuge, an entirely safe refuge. Then his voice changed – the subdued manner was gone – the tremulous tone disappeared. In accents of exultation he proclaimed a divinely glorious Savior. As the fires of Christian triumph flashed from his eyes and flamed forth in his words the hearts of all God's people were kindled in the joy of His salvation, and tears of gratitude coursed down every cheek.

Just then, in a voice loud and thrilling, he cried, 'O, sinners, dear dying sinners, this is our Savior. Come to Him just as you are. Come to Him right now.' In an instant every impenitent person in the house (with a single exception) rose up and rushed forward to the foot of the pulpit. Some outside dashed through the windows to reach the same place. Suddenly there came a strange hush over the house. I expected Dr. Girardeau to lead in prayer or make an earnest exhortation. But no! In clear, sweet and ringing tones he began to sing the well known hymn, 'Come to Jesus.' Ere the hymn was finished there was joy in two worlds. In God's glorious heaven angels were singing and saying, 'He has saved them.' In the rude country church sinners were singing and saying, 'He hath saved *me*.'[43]

When Girardeau pressed sinners to come to the Lord, we are not to think that he had somehow slipped into an Arminian methodology. He called them to come to the *Lord*, not to the *front* of the church. He is self-consciously Calvinist here, for the glorious offer he presents is based squarely on the scriptural teaching of the order of salvation. In one of his sermons he deals with the objection that it can do no good for an unconverted person to pray to God to save him, since the prayers of sinners could not be acceptable to a holy God. Hear his answer:

The explanation is that Jesus, the great High Priest, presents His blood in their behalf, sues out pardon for them by His availing intercessions, and secures for them the grace of the Holy Spirit who, coming in the first instance, not in answer to their prayers, but to the prayers of the great Mediator, awakens in them a sense of their spiritual wants, impels them to pray for divine help, and enables them while struggling in supplication to believe in the person and trust in the merits of the Savior. The people of God, while in their unconverted and ungodly condition, are accepted not because of the efficacy of their prayers, but because Jesus has previously prayed for them. This is the encouragement which the unconverted sinner has in attempting to pray.[44]

In another sermon, Girardeau makes the same point in a more technically theological way:

. . . in the covenant of grace, believers are united to Christ as their federal head. This legal union, however, under a federal constitution does not take effect upon the sinner until he is also *spiritually* united to Christ. This is done by the efficacious grace of the Spirit implanting in his heart a new principle of holiness, the prime element of which is *Faith*. By means of this faith the sinner is enabled to apprehend Christ and to receive the righteousness which He has provided for all His federal constituents. Faith is the instrumental medium by which the sinner becomes an actual partaker of the federal union with all its inestimable blessings.

The moment of the *spiritual* is the precise moment at which the federal relation takes effect, and at which its influence upon the sinner begins to be developed. That instant the ungodly sinner becomes a justified and accepted believer. *His state is changed*. He has passed from a legal state of condemnation and bondage to a legal state of justification and freedom. By virtue of this federal and spiritual union he becomes mystically but truly and really *one* with the Lord Jesus Christ.[45]

This last quotation opens for us another of the great themes of Girardeau's preaching, one to which he constantly returned because he saw it as crucial to a vital experience of Christianity: the union of the believer with Christ. Here again, Girardeau was a true son of John Calvin, for as Ronald S. Wallace's *Calvin's Doctrine of the Christian Life* demonstrates, the reality and implications of mystical union with Christ are absolutely central to all Calvin has to say about living the Christian life in this world. Dr William C. Robinson, in *Columbia Seminary and the Southern Presbyterian Church, 1831–1931*, indicates that there has been a division among Presbyterian theologians on this important matter. Thornwell and Girardeau followed Calvin at this point (which, I believe, is the best interpretation of the Pauline theology).[46] John B. Adger in his *Life and Times* defends Thornwell's and Calvin's teaching here, and also takes their part (over against Hodge and Cunningham) in their related teaching of the real spiritual presence of Christ in the Lord's Supper.[47]

Girardeau's address in 1881 at the semi-centennial celebration of Columbia Seminary on the question of the implications of the federal headship of Christ had much to say about the believer's union with his Savior.[48] I would suggest that his profound grasp of this doctrine which underlay his preaching all through the years had much to do with the existential vitality and soul-moving tenderness of his sermons. Preaching on the relationship between the vine and the branches, Girardeau says:

As long as the branch is united to the vine the vital juices which constitute the life and vigor of the parent stock are by natural processes conveyed to it. Its life depends on its connection with the vine . . . In like manner the church, sustaining an intimate union to Christ, derives from Him those vital influences without which she could not for a moment exist in her spiritual integrity and power.

. . . In consequence of the connection existing between them, the vital influence descending from the head is communicated to the body, pervades every member and secures the regular and healthful discharge of all the bodily functions . . . He is the head of which she is the mystical, but real body. A living influence, an operative energy flows down from Him to the church, diffuses itself through her whole being, animates all her members, and enables her to accomplish all those salutary ministries for which her very existence was designed.[49]

He goes on to explain that the bond of this union is the Holy Spirit:

The Spirit thus dwelling in Christ, comes down with the commission of the exalted Redeemer, endorsed, so to speak, with the seal of the Father, and by His new-creating energy communicates a new life – the life of Christ – to the dead sinner, empowers him to exercise faith in the Son of God and constitutes a vital relation between him and his Savior. Then establishing His permanent residence in the believer, the Spirit sanctifies him in Christ Jesus, forms in him Christ the hope of glory, assimilates him to the image of Christ and endues him with the strength of Christ through which, though impotent in himself, he is enabled to 'do all things.' The believer thus united to Christ becomes one of His members.[50]

Elsewhere, he applies this doctrine with the profoundest encouragement to the embattled believer:

Exalted as He now is . . . He identifies himself with the meanest of His people, and makes common cause with them as they wrestle with the world, the flesh and the Devil. From the throne of glory, as once He did from the mount of transfiguration, He comes down to the low plane of their conflicts, difficulties and woes, and takes their part and bears a hand with them in their hopeless struggle against odds. As old

John Owen in effect says, He appears upon the scene, plants himself on their side, and challenges their adversaries with the demand, 'What question ye with them?' Hands off! These are my brethren, these are my Father's children . . . If ye have anything against them, deal with me; I am here to answer for them. What is done to them is done to me.[51]

Like Calvin before him, Girardeau has the psychological insight to realize that this doctrine is not easy for the human mind to understand: 'This is almost incredible to us circumstanced as we now are . . . it is a tax upon our faith to admit the oneness of so glorious a Savior with ourselves.'[52] How then can our poor mortal minds make sense of and benefit from such exalted truth? His answer to this leads us to another major theme of both his theological work and his preaching: the inner witness of the Spirit of adoption to the child of God. In this context he says: 'It requires the assuring witness of His Spirit to scatter our doubts and convince us that He acknowledges us as His brethren, the adopted children of His Father . . .'[53]

It has long been noted that Girardeau and others he influenced (such as his son-in-law, R. A. Webb) wrote and preached with an unusual fullness on adoption in order to fill out what they considered a gap in the Princeton theology of Hodge and the Union Seminary theology of Dabney.[54] Girardeau for instance believed – and, exegetically speaking, I think he was right – that Dabney had missed some vitally important spiritual truth when he identified adoption with justification.[55] It appears then that those in the Reformed tradition who stress the reality of adoption do so because of their strong grasp of the foundational doctrine of the union of the believer with Christ. Some of the writings of Professor John Murray are certainly an illustration of this connection between the two doctrines.[56] And conversely, those who have little regard for the actuality of union with Christ have correspondingly little to say about adoption.

Girardeau's preaching leaves us in no doubt about the connection between these two related doctrines:

By virtue of this union with Christ we are adopted into the family of God, and being brethren of Christ, become sons of God and joint-heirs with Christ to a glorious inheritance. Without the spirit of adoption it is impossible to serve God acceptably . . . It is only when we cry Abba, Father, only when we approach Him as reconciled through the blood of His Son, that we are enabled to bring forth the peaceable fruits of righteousness. The twinges of conscience, the stings of remorse, and the alarming dread of Hell can never be the motives of a truly sober, righteous, and godly life. The spirit by which we become followers of God as dear children, coupled with a sense of pardon and reconciliation with Him through the blood of Jesus Christ, are absolutely necessary to holiness in life and peace in death.[57]

Nearly all of the other great themes of Girardeau's preaching flow from these central doctrines just discussed. We may summarize most of the remainder of his preaching as his tracing the outflow of the Christian life in various directions, like an explorer or mapmaker following out and charting the varying routes taken by the downcountry branches of a spreading river. His preaching of the Holy Spirit and of personal and ecclesiastical revival has already been discussed. He also had much to say about that great means of grace in the Christian life: prayer. Many believed that one of the most immediately beneficial series he ever preached was on prayer to the defeated, depressed and disillusioned people of Charleston right after the close of the war in late 1865. Dr Girardeau himself says of this series:

Daily prayer was offered by crowds of worshippers for the success of the Confederate struggle. In consequence of its disastrous result, many of God's people were, by Satanic influence, tempted to slack their confidence in prayer. These sermons were an humble attempt to help them under this trial.[58]

One illustration from this series must suffice. Speaking of God's mysterious denial of some of the legitimate supplications (at least from the human viewpoint) of his people, the preacher states:

He may suffer them, for wise purposes, to undergo apparent defeat, and to be exposed to a tempest of opprobrium, oppression and scorn. In these cases it is our duty to sustain ourselves by the consideration that God does His will, and that the Judge of all the earth will do right. And to him who thus in disappointment and suffering, baffled in his hopes, and tempted to skepticism, yet honors God by a meek and uncomplaining submission due from a sinful short-sighted creature, to infinite wisdom and absolute sovereignty, it will in time be made conspicuously to appear – as clearly as the flash of a sunbeam through the fissures of a dissolving cloud – that benefits were withheld for the bestowal of greater, that temporary suffering is but the prelude to everlasting blessing, short-lived disappointment to the dawn of unfading honor, and that truth and right go down beneath a horizon of darkness and an ocean of storms, only to reappear in the morning glory of an eternal triumph.

Jesus as an infirm, dying human being, staggering under the curse of a world, prayed that He might be delivered from suffering the second death. His prayer was unanswered and He died; but His grave was the scene of death's dethronement and the birth-place of unnumbered millions of deathless souls redeemed from Satan, sin and hell. Hold, Christian brother! Do not despair because your prayers for certain blessings . . . have for a time been unanswered. Where is your faith? Where is your allegiance to your almighty, all- wise, all-merciful Sovereign?

Collect yourself. Put on the panoply of God . . . Look up. God, your redeemer and deliverer, reigns. See, He sits on yonder throne, and suns and systems of light are but the sparkling dust beneath his feet. Thousands of thousands of shining seraphs minister before Him. Infinite empire is in His grasp . . . His eye is upon His afflicted people. See, see, He comes, He comes, riding upon the wings of the whirlwind, wielding His glittering sword bathed in the radiance of heaven, driving His foes like chaff before His face, and hastening to the succor of His saints with resources of boundless power and illimitable grace.[59]

A constellation of themes in Girardeau's preaching gathers around the subject of discipline in the Christian life. He preached on how to raise children,[60] and the importance of family worship.[61] Many were his sermons against worldliness.[62] He wisely saw, however, that there is a right way and a wrong way to preach against sin, and that therefore one 'must shrink from assuming the office of a censorious critic of the church . . .'[63]

In addition, he preached many messages of an apologetic nature in order to strengthen the intellectual and moral resolve of God's people under the increasing onslaught of humanist rationalism in the late nineteenth century. This too is connected to the central issue of the Christian life. It is his way of reminding his hearers that God, the soul of man and the eternal spiritual world are utterly real, and that nothing matters so much as having one's soul put right with God through receiving the atonement of Christ and that 'spirit which answers to the blood, and tells me I am born of God.' Under this same aspect of the eternal importance of spiritual reality, and specifically the Christian life viewed in its final outcome, is to be placed his considerable amount of preaching on the world to come and the Last Judgment. All of these varying themes are, like the branches of a river from mountainous headwaters, the direct outflow of the primary and central subject of his preaching: 'Jesus Christ, and him crucified.'

16

EFFECTIVE SERMONS: THEIR NATURE AND POWER

Our study of the technical details of the structure of Girardeau's preaching must be all too brief and far from satisfying to us for two reasons. First, he left very few printed sermons (only one volume), and his friends said these were far from his best. Second, his editors also tell us that even when he wrote out a manuscript, his actual delivery of the message often bore little relation to what was written. That is, not only do these few manuscripts lack the 'thunder and lightning' (to use Whitefield's image), but the actual content, phrases, words and thoughts of his pulpit proclamations were different from what he wrote. Probably several things combined to make him free from dependence upon what he had prepared. The first would have been his desire to communicate effectively to simple audiences, which required direct eye and soul contact. Added to this were his sensitive emotions and powers of ready imagination and, above all, his experience of the Holy Spirit when preaching, which often gave him remarkable powers of ready expression. These deviations from what he had written were therefore highly beneficial. We can well believe those who say that his spoken word was far superior to the written form. If it were not so, based on the written material he has left, it would be hard to see how he could be ranked with Spurgeon. In some of this material there are passages that give us glimpses of highest eloquence and tenderest beauty, but for the most part, the written messages, though better than average, do not impress one as being absolutely first rate.

Having recognized our disadvantages, let us do the best we

can to capture something of the atmosphere of the preaching which so many found inspiring. First, he used his fine mental powers to good advantage. He had remarkable powers of concentration and memorization. Somewhat like Jonathan Edwards (without being of that order of genius), he would think highly complex questions through in his mind without writing down the steps, yet was able to retain the various steps in mind after the problem was solved. This kind of mental exertion helped him in his pulpit preparations, which were very thorough and exegetically precise. That Girardeau preached without notes does not mean he had made no notes. He was not a preacher who waited for the inspiration of the moment without having done serious homework; rather, the contrary.

Secondly, enough scenes from his preaching have been quoted to indicate that he did everything he could to adapt his presentation to the capacity and interest of his audience. Like St Paul, he became all things to all men in order to save some.

From the technical viewpoint, a third feature of his preaching is the vivid, fertile imagination which made him a Rembrandt-like painter with words. We must be content with only a few illustrations of his wonderful gift. In tones like those of Thomas Boston's section on the resurrection in his immortal *Human Nature in its Fourfold State*, Girardeau paints a picture of the resurrection morning:

> The dead are rising! . . . Magnificent mausoleums are bursting in which lie inurned the ashes of sceptered monarchs; moss-covered sepulchers are cleaving, beneath which molder the remains of priests and high-priests, nobles and princes, legislators and warriors, philosophers, orators, and poets; while the grass-grown mounds under which the slave and the peasant repose in death are not disobedient to the heavenly call.
>
> From dim cathedral aisles, from every crowded churchyard, from forest burying grounds, from profoundest ocean depths, the long-forgotten dead are starting into new, immortal being amidst the thrilling realities of the judgment day. The solitary traveler rises from the lonely grave which he found in a land far distant from home; while from the narrow beds in which they slept side by side in the populous cemetery whole families rise together . . . the mother once more clasps in her arms the babe that had slumbered with her in the same grave, and mingled its dust with hers.[64]

In another sermon his imagination pictures the glory of the name of Christ all across the physical and moral universe:

The wonder is that the name of the sinner's Savior is not seen to be inscribed on the heavens above, on the earth beneath, and on the profoundest principles of the human soul. The wonder is, that the man of science does not read it ciphered in starry letters upon the nocturnal sky, and chronicled in every element and force of the physical globe; and that the philosopher, bending the ear of consciousness to the phenomena of inward experience, does not hear it cried out from the lowest depths of his moral being The wonder is, that he does not think as in the shadow of the cross, and write as if his pen were dipped in atoning blood.[65]

Elsewhere, he vividly depicts the meaning of the petition 'lead us not into temptation, but deliver us from evil':

. . . and may defend us from . . . the innumerable dangers . . . to which we are every day and every moment exposed; unless it be so that the internal influence of prayer controls the arrangements of Providence and manages the forces of nature, foils the intelligence and baffles the power of the great Adversary, directs the steps, ties the hands and seals the lips of men, cures the maladies of the body, checks the sweep of the pestilence, arrests the flight of the destroying angel, and converts famine into plenty, war into peace, and death into life.[66]

His presentations of the sufferings of the Savior for sinners were perhaps the most powerful of his theologically profound, yet emotion-charged word pictures – but we have given illustrations of this already, and of the effects it had on his congregations.

Another element in the structure of his preaching, and one closely related to his ability to imagine and then picture vivid scenes to his audience, was his power of contrast – a most useful tool in the workshop of any effective preacher. One example of his skill with this tool must suffice. Preaching on how nature itself manifests the judgment of God, he makes these unusual contrasts:

. . . the elements of nature are not unfrequently made the ministers of destruction to man. The sun, which is at one time the cause of life, is, at another, the occasion of death; the moon blights the eye of the sleeper with its silvery beam; the stars which guide the feet of the benighted wayfarer become obscured with clouds, and mock his wanderings; the ocean which bears the commerce of man on its smooth bosom is lashed by tempests into wrath, and swallows up his hoarded treasures and the dearest objects of his love; the winds, which now breathe with the softness of the zephyr at summer eventide, anon rise into fury and sweep the earth with the besom of destruction . . .[67]

Behind his word painting (and skillful rhetorical contrasts) lay not only a sanctified imagination but a lifetime of wide reading in many subjects across a broad field of culture. His sermons demonstrate a most competent grasp of world history,[68] careful attention to current events on the world scene, in Europe as well as in America,[69] and an unusually thorough knowledge of the history and content of philosophy.[70]

It is probably the case that most of our congregations today would be unable to handle some of the historical, analytical preaching passages in Girardeau's pulpit ministry. Of course nineteenth-century Presbyterian audiences were, as a rule, better grounded in careful logical thinking than we who are products of twentieth-century schools. Even so, we may wonder if the detailed steps in some of his arguments might not sometimes have been rather difficult for a congregation to follow.[71] Martyn Lloyd-Jones in his *Preaching and Preachers* wisely warns us against overly close reasoning.[72] It is true that Thornwell also occasionally preached in the same sort of closely reasoned way, and both men seem to have been well received. Nevertheless, given the generally weak state of our current intellectual culture, it would seem unwise to emulate either of them in this area, much as we may wish to follow them in so many other ways. For example, preachers today might do well to learn from Girardeau that an essential element in any effective sermon is its unity. A look at discussions by both Dabney and Martyn Lloyd-Jones of unity and form in the sermon,[73] followed by a survey of the sermons of Girardeau, will impress the reader with how well he carries out their injunction that the sermon should have unity – in the same way as it is a requirement for a work of art or a symphony.

To use another criterion from Dabney, 'textual fidelity' is absolutely essential to any faithful biblical preacher.[74] Girardeau's sermons were faithful to the biblical text, both in the smaller and larger context of scriptural truth. The way he handles Hebrews chapter 10 is an example of his ability here.[75] Girardeau is also most adept at stating clearly at the beginning of the sermon the doctrinal proposition which the text teaches and which he intends to inculcate, and he also manages to do it in a way that is not pedantic and stiff.[76] His introductions (such as remain to us in his printed works) are certainly appropriate and competent, but I think his conclusions are much more powerful and skillful than his introductions. Here he excels as a mighty orator who is able to command the minds, emotions and wills of men. Sad to say, his sermons which were reported to have had the most visible effects are nearly all unrecorded.

The sermons of Girardeau were marked not only by unity, good introductions and powerful conclusions, but also by a generally well organized outline. A glance at any of his sermons will demonstrate his quality here. His sermons were technically organized in a way that the expositions of John Calvin, for instance, were not. Yet in my opinion, Girardeau's preaching – and that of nearly all of his nineteenth-century evangelical contemporaries – suffers in a different respect in comparison to that of Calvin, Zwingli, Luther and Bullinger. Those men preached sequentially through entire books of Scripture, whereas he, Thornwell, Palmer, Spurgeon and the others, chose various texts or topics from throughout the Bible, rather than regularly working their way through whole books. Something of the divine logic does seem to be lost when the preacher fails to work through an entire book, for the more expository method will generally be better informed by the very sequence and connection of one passage, doctrine and thought with another which follows. Dr Martyn Lloyd-Jones' *Expositions of the Book of Romans* are an excellent illustration of how sequential preaching reveals to us important insights into the divine logic, which then enter into our presentation of the text. Nonetheless, in spite of what – in this author's opinion – is a defect which Girardeau shared with most of his nineteenth-century brethren, there can be no doubt that his selective textual, topical preaching wrought mightily in his generation.

It will have been made clear from our study of Girardeau's life and work that large numbers of people of different races and classes were brought to a saving knowledge of Jesus Christ through his preaching. Psalm 19:7 could well have been emblazoned in letters of light across his pulpit: 'The law of the Lord is perfect, converting the soul.' It is equally clear that countless saints were edified and the church built up through his pulpit ministrations. But not only was Girardeau's preaching blessed in this normal and ordinary way of quietly and regularly edifying the church and saving sinners, his preaching was also attended with an unusual blessing that is granted to few ministers of God in history: heaven-sent revival fell upon the scene of his pulpit and prayer-room labors, as we have seen in 1858 in Charleston. Theologically speaking, we cannot of course say that his preaching and praying caused the revival, for that is a sovereign act of the Triune God, but surely there was some kind of connection between the nature of his praying and preaching and what God graciously granted in 1858. Undoubtedly, a basic principle here is that God gives prayers to his people in order to release prepared blessings. Since the twentieth century is the only century since the great Protestant Reformation that has not yet seen a major revival in the Anglo-Saxon world, should we not ask God to give us a true spirit of supplication and then to grant answers to the supplications that he has engendered within us? Let us pray that we may see revival before another century is upon us.

Another salutary effect of Girardeau's preaching was the widespread dispersal of salt and light in society at large in Low Country, South Carolina. This kind of influence is impossible for a human mind to measure, and this matter is after all reserved for Judgment Day. But here and there we are given hints of the good influence of gospel preaching through the years, and this is true of the preaching of Girardeau. One incident in particular stands out as a potent parable of the power of the gospel and of the way God honored the life and preaching of this man. This important incident should be told in every South Carolina history textbook, but given the secular nature of our school texts, that is not likely for a long time!

I refer to the preservation of the beautiful city of Charleston – of whose historic, colonial beauty and cultured Southern charm we are all so proud – from destruction by seditious burning during the War Between the States. Here is the now forgotten story, which demonstrates the massive power one consecrated pulpit can have in a corrupt society:

. . . Charleston was the citadel of 'Secession,' and as such, detested by the Federal authorities, and most of the people of the North. Not a few of these yearned to see it laid in ashes . . . Several times efforts were made to secretly organize the negroes, and through them to start fires at the same time in many parts of the city. Special agents were employed to carry out such designs, and more than once they almost succeeded.

After the war it became an open secret why these well laid schemes were frustrated. Some leaders of the negroes religiously believed that Dr. Girardeau was the special representative of God to their race; and his church a holy temple in which the Almighty delighted to dwell. They feared, and they imparted this fear to other leaders, that if negroes burned that city so dear to this man of God, and that church so beloved and honored by the Lord of heaven, *then* the divine curse might rest upon them and heaven withhold that freedom which they felt was almost within their grasp. The self-sacrificing work of one man indirectly but really saved 'The City by the Sea.'[77]

If you should ever go to Charleston, take time to thank the Lord for using the ministry of his servant, Girardeau, to preserve that place which has long since forgotten the great preacher to the blacks. It is to his influence that we owe the continuance of such an architectural treasure.

We have surveyed the contents, the structure and the effects of Girardeau's preaching. It remains for us to do our best to penetrate through the mist of the long past years as well as the natural reserve of a humble Christian man to see if we can discover something of the source of his preaching power.

A remark that Robert L. Dabney makes in his *Sacred Rhetoric* gives us, I believe, the key which opens the door into that secret place where we shall find the source of Girardeau's pulpit power: 'the prime qualification of the sacred orator is sincere, eminent piety'.[78] His piety was based upon a vital experience of the saving grace of God in Jesus Christ, an unswerving intellectual and moral commitment to the inerrant truth of Scripture,[79] and an earnest, fervent, continual dedication to personal and corporate prayer.[80] All these issued in an endeavor after universal obedience and the daily keeping of 'short accounts' with the Lord. This kind of life never lacks in results for those who are prepared to pay the price. The scriptural piety which pervaded the experience of Girardeau issued in pulpit unction, which seems to be the ultimate 'engine' that drives the preacher's words home to the heart of the hearer.

The concept of 'unction', then, is probably as far as the human mind can go in tracing the remarkable preaching power of Girardeau. But it is not easy to define unction. The nineteenth-century Methodist devotional writer, E. M. Bounds, while rather weak in his biblical theology of prayer, does have some helpful comments on pulpit unction in his classic *Power Through Prayer*:

> . . . [it is] the indefinable in preaching which makes it preaching . . . that which distinguishes and separates preaching from all mere human address . . . unction is that indefinable, indescribable something which an old, renowned Scottish preacher describes thus: 'There is sometimes somewhat in preaching that cannot be described either to matter or expression, and cannot be described what it is, or from whence it cometh, but with a sweet violence it pierceth into the heart and affections and comes immediately from the Lord; but if there be any way to obtain such a thing it is by the heavenly disposition of the speaker.'
>
> . . .Unction . . . inspires and clarifies his intellect, gives insight and grasp and projecting power; which is greater than head power; and tenderness, purity, force flow from the heart by it. Enlargement, freedom, fullness of thought, directness and simplicity of utterance are the fruits of this unction.[81]

In our own generation and in our own theological tradition, Dr Martyn Lloyd-Jones states it simply and directly: 'You can have knowledge, and you can be meticulous in your preparation; but without the unction of the Holy Spirit you will have no power, and your preaching will not be effective.'[82]

We in the Reformed tradition have quite properly and necessarily reacted strongly against some of the absolutely appalling, unbiblical claims of various Charismatic leaders to have received striking, new revelation directly from God. They make it sound as though their contemporary, personal experiences were equal to the revelation of God in the Holy Scriptures! Far from being what some regard as Calvinistic over attention to theological detail, taking a stand against this sort of claim enters into the defense of the very substance of the faith 'once for all delivered to the saints.' Any assertion of having new, authoritative revelations clearly compromises the apostolic authority of the inspired Scriptures, and eventually the door could be left open for the confusion and loss of the apostolic gospel. Hence, it is appropriate to be deeply grieved over and opposed to this sort of thinking.

Yet, for all the legitimate concern and revulsion, it is possible that in some quarters there is a tendency to indulge in a dangerous overreaction. For instance, there are some who even assert that God does not guide his people directly through providence and through the gentle nudgings of his Holy Spirit, but only intellectually through understanding the general principles of his Word. This is contrary to the doctrine of Calvin (and I believe of the New Testament) on the necessity of the illumination of the Holy Spirit in the believer in order for him to receive the Scriptures. There is also the neglect, if not outright denial, of the direct witness of the Holy Spirit to the spirit of the believer that he is adopted by God. Thus these historic Calvinist beliefs and practices appear to be dismissed by some who fear that they may leave the door open to irrationalism or to the Charismatic movement.

All this has important implications for our discussions of preaching, because such a mentality discounts (or at least appears to discount) any serious seeking after unction. What seems to be happening here is that the work of the Holy Spirit is unconsciously replaced by an inordinate trust in the ability of some particular system of apologetics to convince the hearer of the truth of the gospel. Hence, any doctrine of direct assurance or immediate witness of the Holy Spirit becomes unacceptable because it challenges the completeness and efficacy of one's apologetic system! May the Lord have mercy upon us! Girardeau would have had no use for any who talked in this way! It seems that Girardeau and the whole Southern Presbyterian tradition (at least in its orthodox phase) would agree with Lloyd-Jones that '. . . if you confine all this to the Apostolic era you are leaving very little for us at the present time'.[83] If I am not mistaken, Lloyd-Jones' call to us modern preachers is the very thing

Girardeau would urge upon us, as we seek to learn from him and honor his and our Savior:

This 'unction', this 'anointing', is the supreme thing. Seek it until you have it; be content with nothing less. Go on until you can say, 'And my speech and my preaching was not with enticing words of man's wisdom, but in demonstration of the Spirit and of power.' He is still able to do 'exceeding abundantly above all that we can ask or think.'[84]

God forbid that any theory of apologetics or any fear of Charismatic folly will cause us to lose our precious biblical, Calvinist heritage of a direct, vital sense of the immediate, daily presence, guidance and unction of that Spirit who flows, like rivers of living waters, from the throne of God and of the Lamb. May heaven and earth pass before we lose the same, inexpressibly real experience that our Southern Presbyterian forefathers had of 'Christ in you, the hope of glory' (Col. 1:27). In order to know these things for ourselves, and to convey them with power to our congregations, we must seek the same unction that Girardeau sought and obtained. Such unction and reality from another world is only given to those who, like Girardeau, from early childhood to the grave, experience that death to self which enables the life of Christ to be made manifest in others (as Paul describes in 2 Cor. 4). Such continual dying to self, with the goal, in our own day and place, of reaching needy sinners of every sort and variety with the saving gospel, will surely be honored by the same Triune God who so owned the preaching of his servant to the slaves of Low Country, the students of Columbia, the privates and general of the Confederacy, and the senators of South Carolina.

At the end of our pilgrimage, as men speak of our ministry, may their minds turn, as ours have done in speaking of John L. Girardeau, to the words of him who alone makes preachers:

'The Spirit of the Lord is upon me, because he hath anointed me to preach the gospel to the poor; he hath sent me to heal the brokenhearted, to preach deliverance to the captives, and recovering of sight to the blind, to set at liberty them that are bruised, to preach the acceptable year of the Lord' (Luke 4:18, 19).

EPILOGUE

A CONCLUDING REFLECTION ON THEIR PREACHING AND OURS.

The four men whom we study in this volume consistently 'preached Christ and him crucified' (1 Cor. 2:2) throughout their ministries. But what, we may ask, is special about that? Is this not the central characteristic of evangelical preaching in every generation? Perhaps it is, and certainly it should be. Yet I fear that there is a trend among evangelicals today, of which they may not even be consciously aware, that is leading them in another direction. Without meaning to do so, many of our contemporary speakers and preachers seem to focus their message upon their own experiences in the Christian life and service rather than upon Christ himself. While the discourse is being delivered, one's interest is certainly held captive. However, when some sermons are ended, we find that what grasped the attention was not the person and work of the eternal Christ and other great verities of the Word, for so little time was devoted to them! Instead, all that is retained is the ephemeral and fading – though scintillating – experiences of other humans, whose life, like our own, is but a vapor and lasts but a moment. At the end of the day, other than giving the audience the pleasure of temporary entertainment, and the preacher the pleasure of being closely followed, what is the lasting use of this approach?

Perhaps this shift of focus comes from the valid concern to hold the attention of their audience, which, according to several studies, is increasingly conditioned by frequent television watching to expect rapidly changing scenes of exciting action, rather than a sustained development of thought. Of course no-one should go into the pulpit who is not intensely concerned to gain a hearing with the people, 'for faith cometh by hearing' (Rom. 10:17). And the incarnation of Christ itself teaches us that it is always necessary to take the surrounding culture into account as we present the unchanging truth to it in terms that it can understand. Thus it would be unwise *not* to be aware of the effects on our hearers of the shift from traditional reading to visual media.

Yet I wonder if the effects of television and modern means of communication have not been overrated? Maybe the attention span of ordinary people has not been irrevocably shortened. What hard evidence is there that human nature has significantly changed in the last thirty years as regards the basic powers of a normal mind? Is it, after all, an empirically demonstrated fact that today's congregations cannot follow with profoundest interest and delight solidly presented biblical sermons, which contain much content and require a sustained train of thought? I think there is considerable evidence that congregations of ordinary working people frequently do so.

There is no doubt that, in most cases, an exciting string of stories or impressive portrayals of famous people will gather a crowd more quickly than even a good and lively exposition of the Word of God. But from a pragmatic viewpoint, this kind of excitement has a way of waning in influence over the long run, in that it is subject to the law of diminishing returns. And more importantly, from the biblical viewpoint, mere excitement and entertainment (even churchly entertainment!) are not said to be the divinely appointed means of conversion and sanctification. According to David, it is 'the law of the Lord' which is perfect, 'converting the soul' (Ps. 19:7). Jesus prayed that the Father would 'sanctify his people in truth, for thy word is truth' (John 17:17). The Apostle Paul made it clear that 'it pleased God through the foolishness of preaching to save them that believe' (1 Cor. 1:21).

I would not wish to imply here that there is anything at all wrong with some public reference to experiences of chastening and grace in one's own life or in that of other persons – small or great – whom we know, and in whom we can trace some work of the Lord which is related to the text we are expounding. Prophets and apostles have made such references, and who of us is in a position to criticize them – or any other faithful preacher – for doing so? The real question is why so many good evangelicals, who would give assent to all of the texts quoted above, seem to be devoting *more* of their sermon time to current stories and personal experiences, and *less* to a serious probing of the truths of Scripture with plain application? Of course interesting contemporary stories and apposite personal references can help convey the larger message of the biblical text. The central issue rather is the *focus* of the message and the *inner attitude* of the speaker which determines the direction of that focus. Simply stated, we must always remember to ask ourselves whether the focus of our message is on Christ (and, of course, the divinely inspired text, where he is to be found), or on self.

In the contemporary intellectual and cultural environment, there can often come a powerful temptation to consider ourselves too wise to devote our time to preaching the foolishness of Christ crucified, and too strong to submerge our career in the weakness of God which is so inglorious to the flesh. If we succumb to such pressures, then has not our focus shifted from God and his promises to self and its plans? Two sentences from Professor James Denney of Glasgow, that were framed and mounted on the wall of a Scottish Presbyterian vestry in the early years of this century, still reveal the heart of the matter: 'No man can bear witness to Christ and to himself at the same time. No man can give the impression that he himself is clever and that Christ is mighty to save.'[1]

The four great preachers of this volume were not lacking in the kind of visible fruit which bears inescapable witness to the saving power of Christ. The 'successful results' of their pulpit ministries (though perhaps not the discipline of their self-denying lives!) would probably be the envy of many today whose preaching emphasis is slanted in a very different direction from theirs. This, I think, is precisely where they can so greatly help us, if we will humble ourselves to listen to them. As I survey the focus of the preaching of Baker, Thornwell, Palmer and Girardeau, it is above all this absence of emphasis on self, and in its stead the delighted commitment to proclaiming Christ in the fullness of scriptural truth that distinguishes them from so much that draws attention in the evangelical world today. Let me illustrate specifically what I mean.

Daniel Baker, as we have seen, was once called by a pulpit vacancy committee in Washington, D.C. Although connected with the congregation, but not an official member of the committee, Andrew Jackson, the President of the United States, sent word to Baker that he hoped he would come as the pastor, for he highly regarded his life and preaching. But in all the sermons of Baker, where do you once find him referring to his connection to the President? Undoubtedly a widespread knowledge of this relationship would have been impressive to people and flattering to the preacher/evangelist. But the focus of his heart was on a relationship that he felt was far more impressive and significant for himself and for the public: a saving knowledge of the Lord Jesus Christ. Therefore, he had neither time nor inclination to share with congregations what presidents and governors thought of him. This wise man knew that it was the work of a lifetime to attend to 'the one thing necessary.' Hence the focus of his preaching never veered from the Christ of the Scriptures.

To offer one other example, James H. Thornwell could certainly have made much of the obvious respect in which he was held by John C. Calhoun, former Vice-President of the United States, and then U.S. Senator from South Carolina. Mid-nineteenth-century South Carolina is said to have been nearly obsessed by politics, and what could have been better calculated to gain the respect and ear of its people than to have let them know of the impressive connections of this Columbia preacher? But where in all his published sermons did he once do so? Just read 'Christ the Model of Missionary Service' and you will know why. Instead of basking in the light of powerful political friends in the nation's capital, he was overwhelmed by the glory of the uncreated light which flowed out of the Father's heart and radiated upon him from the face of the Son, who 'loved him and gave himself for him' in order to bring him home at last to the Father's house above. Thus Thornwell focused his preaching where God focused his light. For he knew that the self-sacrifical, missionary movement of God's own Son secured the riches of redemption, and could touch the human heart with a heavenly love that issued in a responding self-sacrifical devotion of life and resources to the cause of spreading the gospel. How could he, who knew so well that the triumph of the gospel on earth was based on self-sacrifice, have ever used his preaching to inflate and parade the very thing that had to be crucified so that the light of the Savior could shine through? Thornwell had seen too much of the real light to give it up for a lesser glory (including self-glory).

It will not require too much reading to show that Palmer and Girardeau stood right where Baker and Thornwell stood: at the very edge of the stage, as close as they could to the curtains which hide self so that the radiance of 'the bright and morning star' could shine unhindered by the pride of human flesh. Those of us who are willing to focus our heart and preaching today where these four preachers of God's grace in the Old South once focused theirs, may well discover to our own joy and delight – as well as that of our congregation – the reason why 'no flesh should glory in God's presence' (1 Cor. 1:29). There is a far greater and more beautiful glory than that of paltry self-pride. It is a glory that instead of destroying the soul which is focused on it, transforms it – and all who see it.

'But we all, with open face beholding as in a glass the glory of the Lord, are changed into the same image from glory to glory, even as by the Spirit of the Lord (2 Cor. 3:18).

NOTES

THE OLD SOUTH: AN INTRODUCTION

[pp. xiii – xxvi]

1. Robert Manson Myers, *A Georgian at Princeton* (New York: Harcourt Brace Jovanovich, 1976). For fuller correspondence of Charles Colcock Jones and his family see Robert Manson Myers, *The Children of Pride: A True Story of Georgia and the Civil War* (New Haven: Yale University Press, 1972).
2. Robert L. Dabney, *A Defense of Virginia and through her of the South*, 1867 (Harrisonburg, Virginia: Sprinkle Publications, 1977).
3. B. M. Palmer, *The Life and Letters of James Henley Thornwell*, 1875 (Edinburgh: Banner of Truth Trust, 1974), p. 422.
4. Sheldon Vanauken, *The Glittering Illusion* (Regnery Gateway: Washington, D.C., 1989), pp. 71, 114.
5. Lord Acton, *Essays in the Liberal Interpretation of History*, Edited and with an introduction by William H. McNeill (The University of Chicago Press: Chicago and London, 1967), p. 45.
6. Ibid., pp. 68, 69.

PART ONE: DANIEL BAKER: EVANGELISM WITH POWER

[pp. 1 – 57]

1. William M. Baker, *The Life and Labors of the Rev. Daniel Baker, D.D.* (Philadelphia, PA: William S. & Alfred Martien, 1858), p. 17.
2. Ibid., p. 19.
3. Ibid., pp. 20, 21.
4. Daniel Baker, *Revival Sermons: Second Series* (Philadelphia, PA: William S. Martien, 1854), pp. 80, 81.
5. William M. Baker, op.cit., pp. 24, 25.
6. Ibid., p. 27.
7. Ibid., pp. 28, 29.
8. Ibid., p. 31.
9. Ibid., pp. 32, 33.
10. Ibid., p. 33.

11. Ibid., pp. 40, 41.
12. Ibid., p. 43.
13. Ibid., pp. 46, 47, 48.
14. Ibid., p. 53.
15. Ibid., p. 69.
16. Ibid., pp. 69, 70, 71.
17. Ibid., pp. 73, 74.
18. Ibid., pp. 74, 75.
19. Ibid., p. 76.
20. Ibid., p. 98.
21. Ibid., pp. 99, 100.
22. Ibid., pp. 98.
23. Ibid., p. 91.
24. Ibid., pp. 91, 92.
25. Ibid., p. 92.
26. Ibid., p. 107.
27. Ibid.
28. D. Baker, op.cit., p. 383.
29. Ibid., p. 384.
30. W. M. Baker, op.cit., p. 111.
31. Ibid.
32. Ibid., p. 115.
33. Lowry Axley, *Holding Aloft the Torch: A History of the Independent Presbyterian Church of Savannah, Georgia* (Savannah, 1958), p. 45.
34. Axley, op.cit., *passim.*
35. W. M. Baker, op.cit., p. 126.
36. Some of these problems are discussed in letters to a ministerial friend, Mr Handy. See W. M. Baker, op.cit., pp. 120ff.
37. Ibid., p. 134.
38. Ibid., p. 141.
39. Ibid., pp. 141, 142.
40. Ibid., pp. 142, 143.
41. Ibid., p. 147.
42. Ibid., p. 150.
43. Ibid., pp. 158, 159.
44. Ibid., pp. 164, 165.
45. Ibid., p. 169.
46. Ibid., p. 193.
47. Ibid., p. 203.
48. As quoted in William H. Benchoff, *Daniel Baker, Pioneer Missionary to Texas: a Thesis* (East Texas Baptist College: Marshall, Texas, 1954), pp. 28, 29.
49. W. M. Baker, op.cit., p. 216.
50. Ibid., p. 229.
51. Ibid.
52. Ibid., p. 297.
53. Ibid., p. 296.
54. Ibid., p. 326.

55. Ibid.
56. Ibid., p. 344.
57. Ibid., p. 384.
58. Ibid.
59. Ibid., p. 384.
60. Benchoff, op.cit., p. 83.
61. W. M. Baker, op.cit., p. 467.
62. Ibid., p. 492.
63. Ibid., p. 495.
64. Ibid., p. 498.
65. Ibid., p. 501.
66. Ibid., pp. 489, 490.
67. Ibid., p. 504.
68. Ibid., pp. 521, 522.
69. Ibid., p. 531.
70. Ibid., pp. 561, 562.
71. Ibid., pp. 569, 570.
72. Ibid., p. 571.
73. Ibid., p. 572.
74. Daniel Baker, *Revival Sermons: First Series* (Philadelphia, PA: William S. Martien, 1855), p. 379.
75. Ibid., p. 191.
76. Ibid., p. 202.
77. Ibid., p. 268.
78. Ibid., p. 270.
79. Ibid.
80. Ibid., pp. 351, 352.
81. D. Baker, *Rev. Ser. II*, pp. 326, 327.
82. W. M. Baker, op.cit., p. 207.
83. Ibid., p. 189. Interestingly, the South Carolina diocese today is still known for its evangelical persuasion.
84. See Iain H. Murray, *The Forgotten Spurgeon* (London: Banner of Truth Trust, 1966), and I. H. Murray, *The Invitation System* (Edinburgh: Banner of Truth Trust, 1967), for a careful discussion of the different theologies lying behind these varying approaches.
85. W. M. Baker, op.cit., pp. 122, 123.
86. Ibid., p. 145.
87. D. Baker, *Rev. Ser. I*, pp. 376, 377.
88. See Benchoff, op.cit., Appendix A, p. 87.
89. W. M. Baker, op.cit., p. 478.
90. Ibid.
91. Baker, *Rev. Ser. I*, pp. 286, 287.
92. *Rev. Ser. II*, pp. 200, 201.
93. *Rev. Ser. I*, p. 97.
94. Ibid., p. 65.
95. *Rev. Ser. II*, p. 213.
96. W. M. Baker, op.cit., p. 517.
97. Ibid., p. 521.

98. Ibid., p. 476.
99. Ibid., p. 475.
100. *Rev. Ser. II*, p. 313. In this context, Baker makes the strange statement, 'I am a Calvinist so called; not that I embrace all the dogmas of the great Genevan divine, but certainly those that are embraced in the standards of our Church . . .' What he meant here, I do not know.
101. W. M. Baker, p. 366.
102. Ibid., p. 170.
103. Ibid., p. 171.
104. Ibid., p. 383.
105. *Rev. Ser. I*, p. 217.
106. Ibid., p. 307ff.
107. W. M. Baker, op.cit., p. 529.
108. See *Rev. Ser. II*, pp. 204ff.
109. Ibid., pp. 305ff.
110. Ibid., p. 145.
111. *Rev. Ser. I*, Sermon III.
112. *Rev. Ser. I*, Sermon X.
113. *Rev. Ser. I*, p. 357.
114. Ibid., pp. 331, 361.
115. Ibid., p. 146.
116. Ibid., pp. 309, 322.
117. *Rev. Ser. I*, pp. 360, 361.
118. *Rev. Ser. II*, pp. 81–88.
119. Ibid., pp. 96, 97, 122.
120. *Rev. Ser. I*, pp. 34, 133, 143.
121. *Rev. Ser. II*, pp. 364–371.
122. W. M. Baker, op.cit., pp. 259, 264, 298.
123. *Rev. Ser. I*, pp. 300, 306, 307.
124. Ibid., p. 247.
125. *Rev. Ser. II*, p. 159.
126. H. A. White, *Southern Presbyterian Leaders* (Richmond, VA: Presbyterian Committee of Publication, 1911), p. 274.
127. John Miller Wells, *Southern Presbyterian Worthies* (Richmond, VA: Presbyterian Committee of Publication, 1936), p. 100.
128. *Rev. Ser. II*, Sermon I.
129. Ibid., Sermon IV.
130. *Rev. Ser. I*, Sermon X.
131. Ibid., p. 315.
132. Ibid., p. 179.

JAMES HENLEY THORNWELL: LOGIC ON FIRE

[pp. 60 – 83]

1. *Thornwell Centennial Addresses: Delivered Before the Synod of South Carolina in the First Presbyterian Church, Columbia, October 23, 24, 1912* (Published by Order of Synod: Spartanburg, S.C., 1913), pp. 16, 17.
2. *The Collected Writings of James Henley Thornwell, Volume 1. Theological, 1875*

(Edinburgh: Banner of Truth Trust, 1974), p. 576.

3. *Thornwell Centennial Addresses*, pp. 6, 7.

4. B. M. Palmer, *Life of Thornwell*, p. 53.

5. James Oscar Farmer, Jr., *The Metaphysical Confederacy: James Henley Thornwell and the Synthesis of Southern Values* (Macon, GA: Mercer University Press, 1986), p. 53.

6. Incidentally, in the biography of Samuel Davies by Pilcher, a similar divinely appointed circumstance is related of the early evangelicals of Virginia, who on their way to ask toleration of the governor in Williamsburg, just happened to spend the night in the home of a man who showed them his copy of the Westminster Confession, which they had never heard of, but immediately adopted as their own. See George W. Pilcher, *Samuel Davies: Apostle of Dissent in Colonial Virginia* (Knoxville: University of Tennessee Press, 1971), pp. 28, 29. Ernest Trice Thompson regards this story as 'almost certainly apocryphal', *Presbyterians in the South* (Richmond, VA: John Knox Press, 1963), vol. 1, p. 52.

7. Ibid., p. 9.

8. Farmer, op.cit., pp. 44, 59, 60.

9. Palmer, op.cit., p. 137.

10. Ibid.

11. Joseph G. Wardlaw, *Genealogy of the Witherspoon Family* (Yorkville, S.C., 1910), pp. 132, 133, as quoted in Farmer, op.cit., p. 55.

12. Palmer, op.cit., p. 137.

13. Ibid., p. 519.

14. Ibid., p. 58.

15. Ibid., p. 393.

16. Ibid., p. 63.

17. Ibid., p. 123.

18. Ibid., p. 62.

19. Ibid.

20. Ibid., p. 350.

21. Ibid., p. 454.

22. *Collected Writings of Thornwell*, Vol. 1, p. 574.

23. Ibid., p. 452.

24. Ibid., p. 442.

25. Ibid., p. 439.

26. Ibid., p. 440.

27. Wm. C. Sistar, ed., *Thornwell Orphanage: Its Principles and Product* (Thornwell Orphanage Printing Committee, 1942), p. 13.

28. B. M. Palmer, *The Life and Letters of James Henley Thornwell* (Richmond, VA: Whittet & Shepperson, 1875), p. 300.

29. Ibid., p. 130.

30. Ibid., p. 551.

31. Ibid.

32. Ibid., pp. 547, 548.

33. *Thornwell Centl. Add.*, p. 22.

34. Morton H. Smith, *Studies in Southern Presbyterian Theology* (Jackson, MS: Presbyterian Reformation Society, 1962), p. 160.

35. *The Collected Writings of Thornwell*, Vol. 2, p. 257.
36. Ibid., p. 97.
37. *The Collected Writings of Thornwell*, Vol. 4, pp. 571, 572.
38. Ibid., Vol. 2, p. 288.
39. For Thornwell on the order of salvation, see ibid., pp. 77, 78, 281, 282, 327.
40. Ibid., p. 419.
41. William C. Robinson, *Columbia Theological Seminary and the Southern Presbyterian Church 1831–1931* (Decatur, GA, 1931), p. 225.
42. e.g. ibid., pp. 464–467.
43. Ibid., pp. 337, 338.
44. Ibid., p. 346.
45. Ibid., p. 360.
46. cf. ibid., pp. 337ff. and 347.
47. cf. ibid., pp. 353, 354.
48. Palmer, op.cit., p. 130.
49. e.g. cf. *Collected Writings of Thornwell*, Vol. 2, p. 454.
50. e.g. cf. ibid., p. 414.
51. e.g. cf. ibid., p. 415.
52. Palmer, op.cit., pp. 132, 133.
53. *Collected Writings of Thornwell*, Vol. 4, p. 558.
54. Palmer, op.cit., p. 550.
55. *Collected Writings of Thornwell*, Vol. 4, p. 558.
56. Ibid., Vol. 2, pp. 310, 473.

PART THREE: BENJAMIN MORGAN PALMER: CAPTURING THE HEART OF NEW ORLEANS

[pp. 87–118]

1. Palmer, *Sermons* (New Orleans: M. Jones Scott, 1875), Vol. I, p. 212.
2. Thomas Cary Johnson, *The Life and Letters of Benjamin Morgan Palmer*, 1906 (Edinburgh: Banner of Truth Trust, 1987), p. 18.
3. John Miller Wells, *Southern Presbyterian Worthies* (Richmond, VA: Presbyterian Committee of Publication, 1936), p. 141.
4. Ibid., p. 143.
5. Ibid.
6. Johnson, op.cit., p. 67.
7. Ibid., p. 651.
8. Ibid.
9. Ibid., p. 400.
10. Ibid., p. 86.
11. Ibid.
12. Ibid., p. 89.
13. Ibid.
14. Ibid.

15. Ibid., p. 91.
16. Ibid., p. 83.
17. B. M. Palmer, *The Broken Home or Lessons in Sorrow*, 1890 (Harrisonburg, VA: Sprinkle Publications, 1981), pp. 12, 13.
18. Ibid., p. 21.
19. Johnson, op.cit., p. 155.
20. Ibid., p. 272.
21. According to sources at Tulane University Library and Hickey's Bibliography of Southern Presbyterian Writings, the New Orleans newspaper published 'a few' of Palmer's sermons before the War Between the States, then two volumes of sermons during the 1870s, and only eight others.
22. Ibid., p. 663.
23. Johnson, op.cit., p. 369.
24. Jack P. Maddex, 'From Theocracy to Spirituality: The Southern Presbyterian Reversal on Church and State' in *Journal of Presbyterian History*, Vol. 54, No. 4, Winter, 1976.

Indeed, in the light of this and other actions by Southern Presbyterian leaders before the 1870s, Professor Jack P. Maddex has proposed a thorough reinterpretation of what this doctrine meant among Southern Calvinists before the Reconstruction years:

> Antebellum Southern Presbyterians did not teach absolute separation of religion from politics, or even church from state. Most of them were pro-slavery social activists, who worked through the church to defend slavery and reform its practice. Their Confederate militancy did not violate any antebellum tradition of pietism. Only during Reconstruction, in drastically altered circumstances, did they take up the cause of a 'non-secular' church – borrowing it from conservative Presbyterians in the border states.

Maddex is well aware of James H. Thornwell's writings on the spirituality of the church, but argues for a more activistic interpretation of it than has been traditionally understood since the 1870s.

25. Ibid., p. 267.
26. Ibid., p. 490.
27. Ibid., p. 600.
28. Ibid., p. 601.
29. Wells, op.cit., p. 151.
30. Ibid., p. 189.
31. Ibid., p. 431.
32. Ibid.
33. Louis Voss, compiler, *Presbyterianism in New Orleans and Adjacent Points 1818–1930* (Presbyterian Board of Publication, Synod of Louisiana, 1931), p. 153.
34. Ibid., p. 157.
35. Ibid., p. 167.
36. Ibid., pp. 167, 168.
37. Ibid., p. 386.
38. Palmer, *Lessons in Sorrow*, pp. 112, 113.
39. Johnson, op.cit., pp. 593, 594.
40. Ibid., pp. 609, 610, 611.

41. Ibid., p. 613.
42. See chapter 48 of Dr C. W. Grafton's manuscript, *History of the Synod of Mississippi*, written for the Synod in 1927 by Grafton. This valuable manuscript is presently being edited for publication by Dr Albert H. Freundt, Jr, Professor of Church History in Reformed Theological Seminary, Jackson, Mississippi.
43. Louis Voss, op.cit., p. 32.
44. Johnson, op.cit., p. 660.
45. Wells, op.cit., p. 162.
46. Johnson, op.cit., p. 661.
47. Morton H. Smith, *Studies in Southern Presbyterian Theology* (Jackson, MS: Presbyterian Reformation Society, 1962), p. 219, referring to R. B. Kuiper's article, 'Scriptural Preaching' in *The Infallible Word*, eds: Stonehouse and Wooley, Presbyterian and Reformed Publishing Company: Philadelphia, PA, 1946).
48. R. B. Kuiper, art.cit., p. 257.
49. Palmer, *Sermons*, Vol. II (New Orleans: Clark & Hofeline, 1876), Nos. XVI & XVII.
50. Ibid., No. XXXVI, p. 451.
51. Ibid., pp. 246, 247.
52. *Sermons*, Vol. II, p. 219.
53. Ibid., p. 117.
54. Ibid., p. 333.
55. Vol. I, pp. 271, 272.
56. Ibid., pp. 313, 314.
57. Ibid., p. 258.
58. Ibid., p. 226.
59. Ibid., pp. 299, 300.
60. Ibid., p. 293. See also p. 211.
61. Vol. II, p. 219.
62. See ibid., Sermon XXXIII, 'Christ's Universal Dominion.'
63. Wells, op.cit., p. 163.
64. Ibid.
65. Palmer, *Sermons*, Vol. I, p. 395.
66. Ibid., p. 454.
67. Ibid., p. 270.
68. Ibid., pp. 265, 385.
69. Ibid., p. 271.
70. cf. ibid., p. 303.
71. Ibid., p. 273.
72. Palmer, *Sermons*, Vol. I, p. 323.

PART FOUR: JOHN L. GIRARDEAU: UNCTION AT WORK

[pp. 121 – 170]

1. George A. Blackburn, ed., *The Life Work of John L. Girardeau* (Columbia, S.C.: The State Company, 1916), p. 15.

2. Ibid., p. 23.
3. Ibid., p. 22.
4. Ibid., pp. 23, 24.
5. Ibid., p. 24.
6. Morton H. Smith, *Studies In Southern Presbyterian Theology* (Jackson, MS: Presbyterian Reformation Society, 1962), pp. 98, 99.
7. E. Brooks Holifield, *The Gentlemen Theologians: American Theology in Southern Culture 1795–1860* (Durham, N.C.: Duke University Press, 1978), p. 50. See especially Chapter 3, 'The Vanishing Liberals.'
8. Blackburn, ed., op.cit., p. 303.
9. John H. Leith, Professor of Theology, Union Theological Seminary, Richmond, Virginia (unpublished paper), 'The Theological Stance of the Presbyterian Church in the United States,' p. 3.
10. Blackburn, ed., op.cit., p. 61.
11. 'Letter from the Lower Right' (article) by John Shelton Reed, quoting Richard Adler in *Chronicles: A Magazine of American Culture*, Vol. II, No. 4, April, 1987, p. 39.
12. Blackburn, ed., op.cit., pp. 76, 77.
13. Ibid., p. 78.
14. Ibid., p. 87.
15. John N. Akers, *Slavery and Sectionalism: Some Aspects of Church and Society Among Presbyterians in the American South, 1789–1861* (Unpublished Ph.D Dissertation, Edinburgh University, 1973), p. 416.
16. Blackburn, ed., op.cit., p. 61.
17. Ibid., pp. 253, 256.
18. Ibid., pp. 175, 176.
19. Ibid., pp. 173, 174.
20. Ibid., pp. 368, 369.
21. Ibid., pp. 390, 391.
22. Ibid., p. 52.
23. Ibid., p. 57.
24. Ibid., pp. 54, 55.
25. *Sermons by John L. Girardeau*, George A. Blackburn, ed. (Columbia, S.C.: The State Company, 1907), p. 312.
26. Blackburn, ed., op.cit., p. 58.
27. Ibid., pp. 208, 209.
28. Ibid., p. 389.
29. Ibid., p. 137.
30. Ibid., p. 366.
31. D. Martyn Lloyd-Jones, *Preaching and Preachers* (Grand Rapids, MI: Zondervan Publishing House, 1976), p. 58.
32. Blackburn, ed., op.cit., p. 390.
33. Ibid.
34. Ibid., p. 104.
35. Ibid., p. 71.
36. Ibid., p. 384.
37. Ibid., p. 52.
38. *Sermons of Girardeau*, pp. 172ff.

39. Blackburn, ed., op.cit., pp. 52, 53.
40. Ibid., p. 373.
41. Morton H. Smith in David F. Wells, ed., *Reformed Theology in America* (Grand Rapids, MI: Wm. B. Eerdmans, 1985), p. 203.
42. Blackburn, op.cit., p. 128.
43. Ibid., pp. 53, 54.
44. *Sermons of Girardeau*, pp. 295, 296.
45. Ibid., p. 43.
46. William Childs Robinson, *Columbia Theological Seminary and the Southern Presbyterian Church 1831–1931* (Wm. C. Robinson: Columbia Theological Seminary, 1931), pp. 97ff.
47. John B. Adger, *My Life and Times, 1810–1899* (Richmond, VA: Presbyterian Committee of Publication, 1899), pp. 310–326.
48. John L. Girardeau, 'The Federal Theology: Its Import and its Regulative Influence,' in *Memorial Volume of the Semi-Centennial of the Theological Seminary at Columbia, S.C.* (Columbia, S.C.: Presbyterian Publishing House, 1884), pp. 96–128.
49. *Sermons of Girardeau*, pp. 221, 222.
50. Ibid., pp. 223, 224.
51. Ibid., p. 85.
52. Ibid., p. 84.
53. Ibid.
54. Robinson, op.cit., pp. 216–218.
55. Blackburn, ed., op.cit., p. 367.
56. John Murray, *Principles of Conduct* (Grand Rapids, MI: Wm. B. Eerdmans Publ. Co., 1957), pp. 202–228; *The Epistle to the Romans, The New International Commentary on the New Testament* (Grand Rapids, MI: Wm. B. Eerdmans Publ. Co., 1971), chapter 6, ad.loc.; *Collected Writings of John Murray: Vol. 2 – Systematic Theology* (Edinburgh: Banner of Truth Trust, 1977), chapters 21, 22, 23, 24.
57. *Sermons of Girardeau*, pp. 58, 59.
58. Ibid., p. 254.
59. Ibid., pp. 264, 265.
60. Ibid., pp. 160, 162.
61. Ibid., pp. 166, 167.
62. Ibid., p. 169.
63. Ibid., p. 113.
64. Ibid., p. 29.
65. Ibid., p. 83.
66. Ibid., p. 307.
67. Ibid., p. 201.
68. e.g. ibid., pp. 118–120.
69. e.g. ibid., pp. 125, 126.
70. e.g. ibid., pp. 107–109.
71. e.g. ibid., pp. 74–76.
72. Lloyd-Jones, op.cit., p. 223.
73. Robert L. Dabney, *Sacred Rhetoric, 1870* (Edinburgh: Banner of Truth Trust, 1979), pp. 108–114; Lloyd-Jones, op.cit., pp. 72, 73.

74. Dabney, op.cit., pp. 105–108.
75. *Sermons of Girardeau*, pp. 261ff.
76. e.g. Ibid., pp. 172, 254, 369, etc.
77. Blackburn, op.cit., pp. 66, 67.
78. Dabney, op.cit., p. 40.
79. John L. Girardeau, *Discussions of Theological Questions* (Richmond, VA: Presbyterian Committee of Publication, 1905), chapters on 'The Inspiration of the Scriptures' and 'The Authority of the Scriptures,' pp. 273–392.
80. Blackburn, op.cit., pp. 37, 89, 98, 99.
81. Bounds, E. M. (Chicago: Moody Press), pp. 68, 69.
82. Lloyd-Jones, op.cit., p. 319.
83. Ibid., p. 314.
84. Ibid., p. 325.

EPILOGUE: A CONCLUDING REFLECTION ON THEIR PREACHING AND OURS

[pp. 171–175]

1. Quoted in John Reed Miller, *A Pastor's Perspective on Preaching – After Fifty Years: The John Reed Miller Lectures at Reformed Theological Seminary* (Jackson, MS: Evangelical Pulpit Publications, 1988), p. 27.

INDEX

In order to avoid confusion with geographical terms, the words 'The South' or 'Southern' when applied to the old Confederate States appear in italics in this index. Also, the entries for the four main characters of the book begin with biographical references, in the chronological order of the subject's life, followed by other topics and opinions relating to the subject set-out in alphabetical order. Dates have been supplied wherever possible to show the degree of contemporaneity of individuals, though they have been omitted for those where literary or other fame (e.g. Shakespeare, Milton, Scott) would render them superfluous.